'Workers are more precarious than ever as we face the global threats of climate emergency, a creeping far right, increasing inequality, and eroded workers' rights. *Unions Renewed* is a must-read for all in the labour movement who believe that winning working-class power extends beyond government, and must be built from organizing in our communities and workplaces, democratizing our economy and, necessarily, our trade unions. Taking inspiration from a new generation of grassroots unions and movements, the labour movement must radically reimagine itself to take on twenty-first-century capitalism.'

Nadia Whittome, care worker and Labour MP for Nottingham East

'The financialization of the economy has concentrated wealth and power in the hands of the super-rich, devastating workers' living standards, weakening unions and threatening democracy itself. In one of the best simple explanations of financialization I have seen, *Unions Renewed* dissects how private equity corporations profit while bankrupting companies and destroying jobs. It calls on unions to develop new strategies to rebuild workers' power based on how the economy has been reorganized.'

Stephen Lerner, US labour organizer, founder of the Justice for Janitors campaign

'*Unions Renewed* offers a critique of labour's strategic status quo grounded in a clear and powerful analysis of the shifting economic ground beneath us. The authors think both historically and globally – and their insights just keep coming. This book will make a real difference.'

Sam Pizzigati, labour journalist and associate fellow, Institute for Policy Studies, Washington, DC

'The profound social and workforce changes around the dynamics of class, race and gender pose significant challenges, and opportunities, to the trade union movement. To act on this, radical solutions are required which move beyond traditional modes of worker organization. Insights in this important new book shine a light on this changing context and help to chart new pathways to the restoration of trade union legitimacy and power.'

Dr Ian Manborde, Equalities and Diversity Organizer, Equity trade union; former programme coordinator of the MA in International Labour and Trade Union Studies (ILTUS) at Ruskin College, Oxford; founding member of the Coalition of Black Trade Unionists (UK)

'*Unions Renewed* is a clarion call for a stronger, fiercer, better labour movement and it couldn't come at a more important time. While too much of the conversation about the working class is mired in nostalgic dreams of a past that never really was, Martin and Quick have explained why labour must understand the economy that we currently have in order to take power and shape the future. Read it, and then share it with your coworkers.'

Sarah Jaffe, author, *Necessary Trouble: Americans in Revolt* and *Work Won't Love You Back*

Unions Renewed

This book is dedicated to the workers getting us through the COVID-19 pandemic, and to the families and friends of those who have lost their lives in doing so.

Unions Renewed

Building Power in an Age of Finance

Alice Martin
Annie Quick

polity

First published in 2020 by Polity Press

Polity Press
65 Bridge Street
Cambridge CB2 1UR, UK

Polity Press
101 Station Landing
Suite 300
Medford, MA 02155, USA

ISBN-13: 978-1-5095-3911-6
ISBN-13: 978-1-5095-3912-3 (pb)

A catalogue record for this book is available from the British Library.

Library of Congress Cataloging-in-Publication Data

Names: Martin, Alice (Economist), author. | Quick, Annie, author.
Title: Unions renewed : building power in an age of finance / Alice Martin, Annie Quick.
Description: Cambridge, UK ; Medford, MA : Polity Press, 2020. | Includes bibliographical references. | Summary: "Why unions have to reform or die in an age of finance and automation"-- Provided by publisher.
Identifiers: LCCN 2020014208 (print) | LCCN 2020014209 (ebook) | ISBN 9781509539116 (hardback) | ISBN 9781509539123 (paperback) | ISBN 9781509539130 (epub)
Subjects: LCSH: Labor unions--History--21st century. | Labor movement. | Financialization.
Classification: LCC HD6476 .M266 2020 (print) | LCC HD6476 (ebook) | DDC 331.880973--dc23
LC record available at https://lccn.loc.gov/2020014208
LC ebook record available at https://lccn.loc.gov/2020014209

Typeset in 11 on 14 pt Sabon by
Servis Filmsetting Ltd, Stockport, Cheshire
Printed and bound in Great Britain by TJ International Limited

Contents

Acknowledgements

While we were both expecting this project to be a lot of work for us, we didn't realize how much work it would be for other people. We are so indebted to the dozens of people who contributed in various ways. Thank you to Hannah Appel, Christine Berry, Joe Beswick, Gargi Bhattacharyya, Saqib Bhatti, John Burant, Charlie Clarke, Mary Davis, Amardeep Singh Dhillon, Nilufer Erdem, Sian Errington, Miatta Fahnbulleh, Dalia Gebrial, John Goodman, Tony Greenham, Miranda Hall, Aidan Harper, Nadine Houghton, Lydia Hughes, Becca Kirkpatrick, Stephen Lerner, Ian Manborde, Duncan McCann, Charlie MacNamara, John Merrick, Andrew Pendleton, Ann Pettifor, Daniel Randall, Brian Robertson, Vica Rogers, Emily Scurrah, Clifford Singer, Holly Smith, Susie Steed, Lucie Stephens, Beth Stratford, Ravi Subramanian, Lauren Townsend, Andrew Towers, Tod Vachon, Ian Waddell, Hilary Wainwright, Hanna Wheatley, Becki Winson, and George Woods, and to those who chose to remain anonymous for their interviews, discussions, reviews and contributions to the manuscript.

Acknowledgements

We owe particular gratitude to Allison Quick and Matt Phull for their integral input throughout, from helping us think through the big ideas to amending apostrophes on final drafts. Thank you to our editor, George Owers, for his patient reading and advice – and to the anonymous readers for their extremely useful reviews.

All errors or omissions are, of course, our own.

Finally, thank you to our friends and family, especially Matt, Dion and Laura, for keeping us going throughout the process.

Introduction

In 2002 union leader John Antonich of the United Food and Commercial Workers International Union (UFCW) got a phone call. It was from a man whose wife had died after working for Wal-Mart for many years. Antonich explained: 'he told me he got a check for $10,000 from the life insurance company, but Wal-Mart got $40,000'.[1] Why would her employer get any money at all, let alone four times as much as her husband? The answer is that Wal-Mart, like many other major companies, had been taking out life insurance on their employees, often without their knowledge. By the peak of this practice, US companies had spent more than $8 billion on policies covering 6 million workers.[2] They used the insurance premiums to avoid paying tax on a portion of their income, and the policies themselves acted as collateral against which they took out loans.[3] The payout received when the worker died was a mere bonus on an already lucrative practice.

This practice, nicknamed 'dead peasants insurance', is a particularly macabre example of how, in our era of financial capitalism, company owners and financial firms treat workers as another asset to speculate on. If they live, Wal-Mart profits from their labour and secures loans on their backs. If they die, Wal-Mart receives a lump sum. Outraged workers organized against the practice, bringing a series of lawsuits against the company. Wal-Mart, along with the other offenders, wound up the scheme in the early 2000s when the tax loophole which made the practice so lucrative was closed.[4]

Dead peasants insurance is just one case of how workers fare under financialization. Financialization is the trend towards the increased influence of financial actors and motives across the economy. It is capitalism's latest attempt at rent-seeking – the practice of making money from assets, without producing anything in the process. Since the 1980s, the US and the UK have been global trailblazers in financialization, enabling an astonishing increase in the size and influence of the financial sector across the globe. It enables capitalists to extract money from workers in a myriad of ways, not just from selling the services and products they produce. When workers lose their job because their employer focuses all their investments on financial markets instead of productive activity, someone is profiting. When workers get a high-cost loan because their wages won't cover their bills, someone is profiting. Even when workers die, someone may be profiting.

In 2019, however, economic journalist Rana Foroohar announced 'peak Wall Street', warning that the reign of finance may be coming to an end.[5] Even though the 2008 financial crash demonstrated the limitations of the debt-fuelled financial system that caused it, with devastating effect, financialization since then has continued to intensify almost to breaking point.

There are multiple warning signs that this trend has become unsustainable. Personal debt in the US and UK is now higher than before 2008, with increased defaults on car loans spelling particular trouble.[6] At the same time, corporate debt has ballooned, with companies increasingly borrowing not to invest in production, but instead to make money through financial tricks such as share buybacks or financial speculation.[7] Private equity firms – investment management companies whose business model is to buy up companies, load them with debt, and pay themselves handsomely before abandoning the companies to bankruptcy or decline – are often behind the scenes. While financialization has succeeded in making many people very rich for the past few decades, Foroohar argues we are reaching 'the apex of this trend, and there will be diminishing returns for companies that choose to focus more on markets than the real economy'.[8]

There's no question that another financial crash is on its way. The question is whether financialization will be able to limp on through another crisis, or whether it will spell the beginning of the end for this economic era.

The answer will depend in part on whether there is a sustained movement ready to use the opportunity to build something new. Luckily, just as finance is beginning to falter, the labour movement – whose decline since the 1980s has mirrored finance's rise – is showing signs of recovery.

In 2018 more workers went on strike in the US than in any year since the mid-1980s.[9] Led by teachers and General Motors workers, almost 500,000 walked out – some for weeks at a time – in disputes over their poor treatment, and the poor treatment of their communities, by their employers. This increase in militancy marks a significant shift away from the trend that has seen unions in retreat for almost half a century.

As well as improvements in some numbers, there is also a new energy emerging in pockets of the union movement today. In the US and UK workers are returning to some of the more militant and creative activity of unions past, reimagined and recreated to tackle the particular challenges of today. These actions are often being led by the most marginalized workers, often women, migrants and people of colour acting outside existing union hierarchies. A new, unapologetic radicalism has been encapsulated by the wave of US teachers' strikes which has sent ripples of inspiration through the US labour movement, while new unions and branches have sprung up in the UK with an explicit focus on organizing insecure and outsourced workers. Meanwhile, the movement for union renewal is reflected in, and feeding off, the rise in progressive party politics, with democratic socialist candidates in the US and UK elections mobilizing historic numbers of activists and supporters (particularly young people) towards a pro-labour agenda. A new generation of politicized workers is demanding more from unions, including a more coherent response to climate change, and is revisiting historic demands such as a shorter working week. Rather than a dying movement, the union movement could be a giant beginning to awaken.

However, to be successful, this renewal needs to be smart and strategic. A crucial element of this is knowing the enemy. It is the argument of this book (explored in chapter 1) that financialization has profoundly impacted the ability of workers to organize and win in the workplace. As shareholders, private equity firms or financially driven executives find ways to make short-term returns through financial speculation, workers find themselves increasingly side-lined. Wealth creation is occurring not only on the factory floor, but increasingly in property markets, in currency trading or on the stock exchange – areas of the economy which are fuelling runaway inequality but in which the labour movement currently has little, if any, reach. Under these conditions, while traditional workplace wage-bargaining can win important improvements for many workers, it will struggle to achieve a substantial reduction in inequality or shift in economic power.

Now, as financialization looks as though it may begin to falter, the union movement needs a direct strategy for how to bring this era to an end, and usher in a better alternative. To do this, unions must revisit the question of what they are for.

Building economic democracy under financial capitalism

Financial capitalism is, at its heart, about an imbalance of power. One of the ironies of modern neoliberalism is that, while its proponents moralize endlessly about *political* democracy, we effectively live in *economic* dictatorships, where even elected politicians struggle to reign in the power of financial and corporate elites. And yet, without economic democracy, political democracy is a farce.

Under financial capitalism we are disempowered in the deepest sense. Not only are our economic lives strictly constrained by the financial system, but often we don't even understand how these constraints operate or who is behind them. Just like any system of oppression, financial capitalism includes entrenched relationships of authority and subordination, resulting in fundamentally different levels of freedom for different people.

The aim of economic democracy has threaded through past union struggles, and under financial capitalism it becomes even more important. Economic democracy is about moving power for economic decision-making from those who own capital to a much broader group – the workers, renters and carers, from whom capital owners profit. It's about taking collective control over our economic lives – including our working lives and our daily economic decisions – as well as influence over decision-making power in the whole economy.

To the extent that they build the collective power of workers against employers, the owners of companies and sometimes the state, unions are inherently agents of economic democracy. But in the face of financialization, this aim could become more ambitious and expansive.

Unions can build economic democracy in different ways. One way (explored in chapter 2) is by building institutional and political power such that unions can, alongside business, have a more formal role in government decision-making. By having a seat at the table, they can encourage policies more favourable to labour and negotiate on the wages and conditions of workers across whole sectors at a time. This kind of 'institutional power' was built and used in the post-war years, and still operates, albeit in a diluted form, across much of Western Europe. Ultimately, however, this model has failed to stem the vast economic imbalances of financial capitalism and is now in international decline.

Alternatively, unions can play a role in resisting financial extraction where it occurs (explored in chapter 3). This happens first and foremost through workplace organizing and strike action. Under financial capitalism, workers are getting smarter about how to maximize their power, demanding more in negotiations where they do have leverage, and identifying and exposing the real financial interests that lie behind workplace decisions. Workers are also maximizing their numbers by mobilizing *all* those who will be affected by those decisions, including outsourced workers and the wider communities surrounding a workplace. Finally, people are finding ways to resist economic extraction *outside* the workplace, including as shareholders, renters and debtors.

As well as resisting oppression in the current economic system, unions are also building new forms of democratic ownership (explored in chapter 4). By democratizing the means of production, workers have the ability to cut off the opportunity for rent-seeking at source. While unions have a mixed history with collective ownership, they are well placed today to be a force in building worker co-ops, and invest in sectors – such as the 'foundational' economy of our everyday lives – and regions that have been side-lined by finance. Over decades, union-led co-operative projects have provided decent jobs in crucial sectors such as care, and transformed the housing market in areas of New York. But these don't have to be side-shows to the 'main' economy. While some union attempts to democratize ownership on a large scale, such as the Swedish Meidner

Plan and the British Lucas Plan, have been unsuccessful, the cracks in the current financialized economy present opportunities to revisit these bold ideas. As debt-laden firms falter, there is an opportunity for workers to take over parts of the economy we most depend on, and run them in the interests of workers and the wider society.

As unions shift from managing their own decline to shaping and building a new economic system, they can also be bolder about transforming the kind of work we do. This includes reducing working hours, taking a proactive role in transitioning away from damaging or useless work, and shaping new jobs in urgently needed areas of the economy, such as care and renewable energy.

Economic democracy is both a process and a destination. It is possible to build elements of economic democracy here, now, in ways that will improve things immediately. It also offers a broad and optimistic vision for an ambitious political future. Unlike the state-led socialism of much of the twentieth century, economic democracy gives meaning to the 'democratic' in democratic socialism. People are not the passive receivers of publicly provided services and benefits, but active participants in democratic decision-making across different realms, including the structures of the welfare state, in the home or in the workplace.

Economic democracy is the antidote to financialization. As the cracks in financialization begin to appear, there is an opportunity to force more transparency, collective voice and worker control over more areas of the economy. By shifting to the front foot, the labour movement can start laying the groundwork for a new, post-financialized economic system.

The scope of this book

This book is intended for anyone interested in, or working towards, union renewal and economic justice today. Its geographical focus is the UK and the US, though some of the discussion will also resonate with other Anglo-American countries. This focus is because our own experience as UK residents forms the basis of our knowledge, and because workers in the UK and the US are facing similar challenges in relation to neoliberalism, financialization and union decline, meaning that the US provides many useful examples and comparisons. This focus should not suggest that union renewal in these countries is by any means leading the way or worthy of particular attention (indeed, as we write, Indian workers are staging what is possibly the largest strike in human history), or that they are facing uniquely difficult challenges, but is merely a reflection of the authors' own backgrounds and a need to set some manageable boundaries. The research has been informed by conversations with union organizers and members working today, predominantly in the UK, but also in the US. These are included as quotes, and inform the arguments and conclusions we have drawn.

There has been a useful recent revival in literature focused on the craft and strategies of union *organizing* – most notably that of union organizer Jane McAlevey. This work is crucial to any revival of union power, and all the solutions in this book rely on deep, sustained organizing, both inside and outside the workplace.

Rather than focusing on *how* to organize for power within unions, this book instead focuses on how to *use* that power to maximum effect within financialized capitalism. By offering an economic analysis of how financial capitalism is reducing the power of workers, and exploring how workers are resisting it, this book aims to contribute to union strategies intended to transform the economy. While the ideas proposed won't be quick or easy, few of them are new. The seeds of union renewal are already sown, either in unions' history or by today's workers who, coming up against finance, are finding ways to resist it.

The way ahead

None of this will be easy. Unions are starting from a severely weakened base. In the UK, 23 per cent of employees are in a union, about half the level of 1979. While in 1979, four in five people had their wages and conditions set through collective bargaining, today it's just one in five.[10] In the US only 10 per cent of the labour force are in unions, half that of the early 1980s, and in the private sector it's just over 6 per cent.[11] Decades of neoliberalism have atomized our communities and left us isolated. Ferocious union-busting from companies themselves and from the governments in their pockets have stripped unions' rights. Xenophobic propaganda is dividing us against each other.

Meanwhile, finance is a formidable opponent. Its tactics are often hidden, complex and ruthless. But capital has always been this way. The labour movement was built under much more challenging circumstances, where workers risked – and often lost – their lives to organize for a better deal for themselves, their colleagues and their families. It's common to hear the lament that workers in our modern context of insecure work are 'unorganizable'. But the only reason *any* work is secure is that *insecure* workers once organized for it.

Progress will be hard won, as any progress worth having always is. As trade union organizer Jane McAlevey put it, there are 'no shortcuts'. But there is also no alternative.

1

How financialization undermines the power of workers

In August 2018, Tops Friendly Markets, a supermarket chain operating in the north-eastern states of the US, announced the closure of ten of its stores as part of a bankruptcy plan.[1] At the time, the firm had 14,800 employees, over 80 per cent represented by two unions – United Food and Commercial Workers International Union (UFCW) and the Teamsters. The company used the restructuring process to substantially reduce the pension benefits for its workers by withdrawing from the unions' pension plans.[2] The unions eventually approved the reduction, with UFCW union president Frank DeRiso explaining 'it was a bad situation. We've done our part to keep this company in business.'[3]

On the surface, Tops sounds like a textbook case of business failure. In a competitive market, some businesses fail, and when that happens, both owners and workers lose out. Right?

Wrong. Tops' bankruptcy was not the result of inevitable market forces. Tops was driven to bankruptcy by private equity firm Morgan Stanley, which had bought it eleven years earlier in 2007. As the new owners, Morgan

Stanley had loaded the company with over $700 million of debt – more than twice the company's original purchase price, including $377 million borrowed just to pay Morgan Stanley and its investors' dividends on their shares in the company. To be clear, that means they borrowed as much money as the original price of the *entire company*, which they then paid out directly to themselves. When, in 2013, Morgan Stanley sold Tops back to its senior management, it was in so much debt that the new owners simply couldn't make the investments needed to keep the chain competitive.[4]

This story is not unusual. Investigating six other cases of US supermarket chain bankruptcies since 2015, researchers Eileen Appelbaum and Rosemary Batt traced the chains' financial troubles back to a handful of private equity firms.[5] Such firms have been around for decades, but became major economic players in the years preceding the 2008 financial crisis. They take a majority share of private companies – often those in financial trouble, but not always. They usually invest for about five years, and instead of using those investments to upgrade stores, deliver training for employees or improve productivity in other ways, their business model relies on extracting as much money as possible from the company before selling it on. If the company goes broke after, then so be it – they've already cashed in. The strings of grocery store bankruptcies aren't anomalies in the private equity model, they are its logical result.

This presents a particular challenge for workers. There are hundreds of thousands of retail workers across the US whose jobs and conditions are being undermined by these practices. In the classic union model, workers bargain and use strikes to win a higher share of the profits from the owners. But strikes are only threatening if owners need workers to work in order to make money. What if the real people profiting – in this case a private equity firm and their investors – don't *need* to produce anything to make money? What if they can do so through the kind of financial engineering we've seen with Tops Markets?

In this scenario, it's less clear what a strike can achieve. Even Tops workers, with unusually high unionization rates for the private sector, were at a loss. As union president DeRiso explained, 'every collective bargaining process that's been negotiated, we've been in a bad position because of the debt the company has'.[6]

Private equity is just one example of the way in which financialization is changing power dynamics within the labour market. Over the past forty years, the intensification of short-term financial motives across all corners of the economy means that those with capital have found it easier to make money through financial activity than through actually making goods or delivering services. At the same time, it becomes harder for workers to win their share of the pie. This occurs at the level of the workplace; financialization weakens workers' position when bargaining for better wages and conditions, or, indeed, makes it hard to bargain at all. It also occurs at the level of the whole economy; in our current state of financial capitalism, wealth creation is occurring not just through the production of goods and services, but increasingly through real estate, currency trading or private equity markets. It's these practices that are fuelling runaway inequality at the very top. If the labour movement wants to have a role in resisting this, not only through winning increases in wages and conditions, but also through reshaping the economy more broadly, then it has to get more creative and ambitious about how to disrupt the systems of financialization.

We don't claim that financialization is the only economic trend causing trouble for workers; globalization, automation, changes in the kinds of jobs we do and the rise of self-employment all play their part. We take financialization as our focus because it is an important cause that creates distinct problems for the bargaining power of workers – and one that is often overlooked. Perhaps this is unsurprising. Financialization is notoriously hard to get your head around and doesn't make good headlines. A robot stealing your job makes a better cartoon than a private equity firm putting jobs at risk by taking out unsustainable debt.

And yet we need to get our heads around it if we're going to have a chance of seriously redressing economic power imbalances. This book is not another explanation of financialization – there are many good ones out there already. Instead, it's a description of the ways in which financialization is reducing the power that we have over our work and our lives – and how we can resist this.

Finance today: speculative, extractive and rent-seeking

'Finance' simply means economic activities that deal primarily with money itself (rather than making goods or services) and includes banking, investing, lending, borrowing and insurance. While finance has always been part of capitalism, its role has increased so much since the 1980s that the term 'financialization' has been coined to describe this new phase. It's not just that the finance sector is much bigger than it was (although it is). It's also that these institutions, and the people that work in them and benefit from them, are exercising an increasing amount of influence over the rest of the economy.[7]

While it's common to pinpoint the 1980s as the 'start' of financialization, in fact it has been more evolution than revolution. The influence of finance has ebbed and flowed over the past few centuries of British and US history, growing alongside the industrial revolution (particularly in Britain, where it was bolstered by colonialism and slavery),[8] fuelling the Great Depression in the 1930s and being tamed by heavier regulation during the post-war period.[9] Nevertheless, a decisive policy agenda in the 1980s to deregulate finance on both sides of the Atlantic fuelled key shifts that amount to a fundamental change to the way that capitalism works.

Financialization was part of a broader neoliberal agenda ushered in by the Thatcher government in the UK and the Reagan administration in the US. With deregulation, money could flow much more easily across borders, banks were allowed to engage in all sorts of financial activities that were previously forbidden, and financial institutions could charge higher interest on loans. Deregulation also allowed the creation of new types of financial institutions, such as hedge funds and equity funds, forming the 'shadow banking sector'. These became major economic players, but remained largely unregulated.[10] Spawned in the US and the UK, the deregulation agenda was aggressively spread around the world through a combination of 'structural adjustment programmes' (demanding policy change in exchange for international loans), military campaigns and a crucially important export: US-educated economists, who quickly took hold of key financial positions in national and international political and economic institutions.[11]

The results were dramatic. Since the 1980s, finance has grown at a much faster rate than the 'real' economy (the part of the economy that produces goods and services),[12] in both the US and the UK. Its contribution to US national income, for example, more than doubled between 1948 and 2018.[13]

Financialization hasn't just meant more financial activity, it's also meant a different kind. During the post-war era, financial activity often involved direct investments into a particular company. At a global level this took the form of foreign direct investment – when an investor puts money directly into a foreign company, often establishing ownership or a controlling interest in it. It was therefore in the interests of finance to concentrate, for the most part, on pursuing profits in the real economy – in other words, through making and selling useful or desirable things and services as efficiently as possible. For this it is the labour of workers, whether as manufacturers, as sales assistants or in any other role in the value chain of a product or service, which is the primary source of profit.

With deregulation the focus shifted, from *investing* in these types of activities in the real economy towards *speculating* on economic and financial trends. Rather than investing in producing goods and services, the finance sector created more complicated 'financial instruments' (a phrase that should immediately ring alarm bells). They created portfolio investments – 'packages' of many different investments that are sold and resold on the financial markets until the trail back to any genuine underlying asset (a house or company) is almost impossible to trace. Their value can end up far outstripping that of this underlying asset until the house of cards comes falling down, as it did so dramatically in 2007. High-frequency trading is both a symptom and a cause of this trend. While in the 1960s, shares were held for about four years, today the average share is held for around twenty seconds, often bought and sold using algorithms.[14]

You could spend a lifetime trying to understand exactly how these things work – many of the people buying and selling them don't really understand them themselves (the movie *The Big Short* provides a fantastic explanation both of synthetic collateralized debt obligations – the financial instrument that sparked the 2008 financial crisis – and of the astonishing level of ignorance of some of those who traded them). The point is that finance is developing more and more complex ways to make money from existing money without engaging in productive activity in the real economy.

These dynamics are the latest manifestation of capitalism's tendency to create new forms of 'rent-seeking' – the practice of extracting wealth without producing it. The amount of money made through rent-seeking (compared to, for example, creating profits from making and selling cars or coffees) has increased dramatically in recent years – one study estimated that the US has seen an increase from 3 per cent of national income in 1985 to 17 per cent in 2015.[15] That's an increase of over 400 per cent.

Financialization should not be seen as a deviation from 'good, productive' capitalism, but as a natural extension of capitalism's logic. Financial extraction is merely the latest strategy by a capitalist class whose members have been constantly finding ever more ingenious ways to maximize their returns.[16] In doing so they are amassing not just wealth, but power over how the economy runs.

This is because finance has not become detached from the rest of the economy – far from it. What we want to illustrate in this chapter is how the influence of finance runs deeper than it ever has before – into our hospitals and schools through privatization, our homes through mortgages and house-price increases, our household finances through personal debt, and crucially into 'non-financial corporations' as we've seen at Tops – all of which spells trouble for workers.

A changed economic landscape for labour

In various ways, financialization has shifted power away from labour towards capital. One outcome of this has been the decline in the labour share. The labour share (sometimes called the wage share) is the amount of national income (gross domestic product, GDP) that goes to workers, either in wages or as social contributions such as pensions paid by employers. This is compared to the profit share (sometimes called the 'capital share'), which includes profits made by employers (e.g. those paid out to shareholders) as well as other returns on capital, including those made through the 'rent-seeking' activities that are so central to financialization.

Labour shares began trending down in the 1980s across advanced capitalist economies, reaching their lowest level just prior to the global financial crisis of 2008, and in most countries have not recovered much since. The pattern in the US has been particularly marked, with a drop of over 10 per cent between 1970 and 2014.[17] Although worker power is about much more than just wages, a decline in the wage share is a major indicator that things are not going well for workers. It's a sign of *structural* inequality: while wealth owners see returns on their property or shares increase, those without such assets have less and less to go around.[18]

The financialization of the 'real economy'

Under financial capitalism the shops we buy clothes from, the cafés we buy coffee from or even the public services we use are increasingly tangled up with financial markets and motives. As we will endeavour to illustrate in the following sections, financialization of these so-called 'non-financial corporations' has profoundly changed the terrain of workplace bargaining.

Shareholder supremacy

One of the financial motives that has increasingly penetrated non-financial firms is the fetishization of the share price and shareholder returns. A particular variation of the profit motive – the aggressive maximization of short-term returns for shareholders – has become increasingly dominant since the 1980s.[19] Under financialization, firms have shifted away from retaining corporate earnings and reinvesting them in the business (to grow productivity and increase future profits), towards a model of distributing corporate earnings to shareholders, often at the cost of downsizing the workforce or selling off assets.[20]

At times this model has been aggressively imposed by

shareholders themselves. A number of dramatic examples in the 1990s resulted in shareholders deposing chief executive officers (CEOs) at General Motors (GM), IBM, American Express and Coca-Cola who were unwilling to comply with this mantra.[21] More often, however, CEOs are complicit in share-price prioritization. Increasingly, CEOs' salaries are pegged to share prices, or they are rewarded with the option to buy equity themselves, giving them a very direct incentive to do whatever they can to ramp up the share price. This leads to absurd scenarios, such as Tim Steiner, boss of British online shopping company Ocado, pocketing a £54m bonus in 2019, despite the firm posting a bruising £214.5m loss, because the share price (on which his bonus is pegged) had increased.[22]

A particularly cynical indicator of this new order is the practice of share buy-backs, where CEOs use profits to buy back their firm's shares, increasing the share price and thereby their salaries. Between 2014 and 2016, American firms spent an astonishing £7 trillion on buy-backs, equivalent to *half* their profits.[23] With millions of US workers living in poverty, those are profits that could have been spent on increasing wages, training or benefits. This marks a decisive shift in the relationship between industry and stock markets. While shareholders defend stock markets as providing industries with the capital they need in order to grow and invest, economist and former advisor to the UK government John Kay has found that, in both the US and the UK, stock markets no longer primarily act as a means of putting money *into* companies but rather a means of *getting it out*.[24] This is literally the opposite of what the economic textbooks tell us stock markets are supposed to do.

This focus on short-term share prices undermines workers' power in important ways. While managers have always had an interest in limiting the amount spent on wages, this has to be weighed up against retaining a skilled, dedicated workforce that can help build a long-term, profitable business. With CEO salaries linked to share prices, CEOs' interests are more closely aligned with shareholders' towards a 'downsize and distribute' model – downsizing the workforce and distributing profits to shareholders. The quintessential example of this was General Electric CEO Jack Welch, who became famous for a regime in which he sacked the bottom tenth of staff and the bottom tenth of management every year, no matter how good or bad the overall performance of the company.[25]

Increasingly, the management of large companies has become dominated by accountants and MBA graduates with more expertise and interest in the bottom line than in the core activity of the company itself. The truth is that in the short term, this approach works; CEOs of the fifty US firms that laid off the most workers since the onset of the economic crisis took home 42 per cent more money than the average CEO.[26]

With increasing privatization in the UK since the 1980s, the mantra of shareholder supremacy has also penetrated the delivery of public services. The now infamous outsourcing company Carillion had multiple contracts to deliver a raft of UK public services, including across prisons, hospitals and schools. Using a finance technique called 'net present value' Carillion was able to pay shareholders returns based on *expected future cash-flows*. Between 2012 and 2016 the company made a total profit of £669 million and paid out £371 million to shareholders. But in fact, they'd only generated £166.4 million in cash from normal operating activities. That means that, using creative accounting, they paid shareholders *more than twice* the amount they actually made. These practices ultimately hollowed out what was left of any profitable business, until Carillion collapsed in one of the largest liquidations in history, losing thousands of jobs and costing the taxpayer £150 million.[27]

Making money without making things

An increasing number of non-financial corporations make money less through profiting from productive activities than through financial rent-seeking. Often this starts with a company establishing a parallel financial branch offering customers credit in order to buy their products. Soon these financial activities extend into those entirely unrelated to the company's 'core' industrial activity.[28]

These financial activities aren't sideshows; they are widespread and substantial. In 2003 GM and Ford – supposedly two examples of the strength of US manufacturing – registered nearly *all* their profit from consumer leasing arrangements, with the bit of their business that actually makes cars barely breaking even.[29] One Wall Street analyst estimates that in 2000 almost 40 per cent of the earnings of the 500 highest-earning US companies were from lending, trading, venture investments and other financial activities, and a third of this was by non-financial corporations.[30]

This spells a massive shift in the relative power of capital and labour. Workers only have the power to demand higher wages or better conditions if employers need them to work in order to profit. If that's no longer true, this undermines the very basis of labour's structural power. Financial activity effectively offers an 'exit option' for capital in negotiations with workers – a way to make money that bypasses the need to invest in either jobs or wages.

American business journalist Rana Foroohar describes this dynamic in the US pharmaceuticals industry – 'perhaps the most financialized of all' – which cut 150,000 jobs between 2008 and 2016 to focus on 'outsourcing, tax optimisation, inversions and "creative" accounting', in ways that, as Foroohar puts it, 'make them look suspiciously like portfolio management companies'.[31] Airlines too, she points out, 'often make more money from hedging on oil prices than selling seats'.

There's good evidence that increased financial activity of this sort can provide 'exit options' for firms and have had a real impact on labour's bargaining power. One study, looking at non-financial US corporations between 1970 and 2008, found that the more a company depended on financial activities, the smaller the share of their income they paid to workers. This accounted for more than half of the decline in the national labour share – a massive impact on workers' lives. The financialization of non-financial corporations is also associated with bigger salaries for executives, and increased inequality in wages.[32]

Rather than using finance to boost the productive business of a company, financialization often undermines the viability of the whole operation. General Electric (GE) is a classic example of the financialized firm. Its financial arm, GE Capital, was set up to help the company's customers buy its goods using tax-efficient leaseback arrangements, and soon expanded into consumer credit. By 2003, 42 per cent of GE's profits were generated by GE Capital.[33] However, it soon became so big (the US's seventh largest bank) that it was subjected to tougher federal regulation and, as the economy struggled in the aftermath of the 2008 recession, investors became nervous about its volatility. By 2015, GE Capital had become a liability and GE sold it off. GE Capital's failure has contributed to ongoing challenges with the company, and once again it's their 'long-suffering' workers who lost out, with 20,000 workers seeing a pension freeze from 2020.[34] Enron followed a similar trajectory, becoming heavily financialized and finally going bankrupt in 2001, leaving 4,000 workers without jobs.[35]

Indebted on purpose

High levels of corporate debt occur in almost every story of ill-fated corporate financialization. But in many cases, companies aren't borrowing because of difficulties with their core business. Indebtedness has become a deliberate strategy used by companies, borrowing to invest in financial speculation or share buybacks, or to avoid taxes.

The International Monetary Fund (IMF) estimates that, as of 2019, there was almost $19 trillion of 'corporate debt at risk' globally – that is, debt owed by firms unable to cover interest expenses, let alone pay back the actual debt – with US and UK companies some of the most at risk.[36]

The cost of servicing these debts is yet another way in which money moves away from productive activity and workers, and towards the finance sector. With financial deregulation, these payments have increased substantially. In the US, payments from non-financial corporations to financial markets doubled from the mid-1980s to the late 1990s.[37] Although central banks have reduced their 'base' interest rates since 2008, this reduction hasn't necessarily been reflected in the real interest rates paid by businesses, as banks often responded to financial uncertainty with higher risk premiums.[38] These costs are having a very real impact on workers: higher interest rates tend to increase the profit share at the expense of the labour share,[39] and the amount paid by non-financial corporations to financial corporations is one of the most significant factors in reducing the wage share across OECD countries.[40]

It would be a mistake to see company indebtedness as a case of 'good' non-financial companies being fleeced by 'bad' financiers. Rather, the struggle is between capital and the executives whose interests align with it on the one hand, and workers on the other. For example, there is evidence that companies use debt to protect the wealth of their own shareholders from the grasp of their workforce. An indebted company can more easily claim it's unable to pay workers more during wage-bargaining. One study found that firms facing a greater threat of unionization choose a higher debt-to-equity ratio, suggesting indebtedness is intentionally used as a union avoidance strategy.[41]

As we saw with Tops Markets, excessive indebtedness is a favourite tactic of private equity firms, which can load companies up with debt and then don't even need to stick around for the consequences. Toys 'R' Us and Safeway are two more examples that have gone the way of Tops Friendly Markets, with workers bearing the brunt of the pain.[42] As one local union president,

Mark Federici, put it, their model is to 'borrow other people's money to make an acquisition and strip the company you acquire of its assets to pay off your debt, while charging unconscionable, undeserved management fees'.[43]

Private equity firms are particularly pernicious when it comes to intentional indebtedness. In the words of Philip Jennings, general secretary of the UNI Global Union, their philosophy is 'buy it, strip it and flip it . . . It's all about value extraction and not value creation.'[44] Because these firms aren't publicly listed, they don't have to publish information such as annual accounts, leaving unions at a distinct disadvantage in negotiations, where knowledge is often power.[45] While private equity professionals are extremely hostile to workers trying to protect their wages, their own salaries are astronomical – in 2018, 'base' salaries of managing partners in the UK were almost £800k, with bonuses of over a million.[46]

The public sector is also affected by indebtedness under financialization, although the dynamics are different. In 2009, Newham council (a branch of UK local government) in East London took out six loans worth £150m. Rather than borrowing from the government, Newham took a gamble, taking out 'inverse floater lender option borrower option (LOBO) loans' from the Royal Bank of Scotland (RBS) and Barclays Bank. The conditions were that the council would pay a low rate as long as real interest rates rose, and vice versa. When interest rates fell to an historic low post-crash, Newham found itself straddled with a colossal debt burden – at one point paying the equivalent of 110 per cent of its entire council tax income just servicing interest on its debts.[47] During this period, austerity was biting, and local residents and local government workers were being heavily squeezed in what was already one of the most deprived councils in England. Newham is not alone – across Britain, councils owe £11 billion in LOBO loans. When local authorities get sucked into financial gambling and lose, it's tax payers and public sector workers who pay the price.

Outsourcing and subcontracting

The doctrine of maximizing shareholder value has incentivized CEOs to maintain the lightest possible base of assets, including labour. This has involved the widespread use of contractors for manufacturing and distribution – a practice that has come to be called Nikefication, in honour of the firm that pioneered this approach.[48]

Many of the most powerful corporations today do their best to minimize their workforce, maintaining a layer of top management and then outsourcing and subcontracting the rest. In IT, manufacturing, sales, research, cleaning and security services, there are few job functions immune to outsourcing today. Outsourced services can then also be further outsourced or subcontracted in multiple layers, extending beyond borders to overseas workers.

Multiple layers of subcontracting make it hard to bargain for increased wages because your direct employer might only have tiny profit margins. The bulk of profits are syphoned off as you move up the layers of subcontractors. In order to speak to someone who has any real ability to pay you more you have to go straight to the top. But following the money may only get you as far as an obscure company name on a tax haven register, and even if you are able to identify the parent company, your specific group of workers are unlikely to have much sway – after all, if wages push up the costs of that contract, the company can always go with another. Outsourcing breaks up and stratifies workforces, making the formation of a critical mass more difficult.

One of the first examples of workers getting to grips with this challenge was the US Justice for Janitors campaign. Before the 1980s, the building services industry in Los Angeles was largely unionized. Business owners hired and managed their own janitors, making it fairly simple for unions to sign contracts with the manager of a particular building. But with the 1980s, building owners started hiring contractors for janitorial services for their buildings. This presented a massive challenge to workers – if they were successful in pressuring one contractor to sign a union contract, the building owner could simply end the contract with that company and hire a non-unionized contractor instead. Looking back, union organizers Stephen Lerner and Jono Shaffer reflected how the campaign 'exposed an economy that was increasingly using sub-contracting and other schemes to separate and isolate workers from the corporations and companies that were actually in control of their wages, benefits and overall working conditions'.[49] The janitors were ultimately successful (as discussed in chapter 3), but the use of subcontracting presented massive hardships in the meantime for an already low-paid and largely migrant workforce.[50]

Subcontracting and outsourcing is a key way in which financial interests wheedle their way into public finances. In the UK in the 1990s, a series of public–private partnership agreements began outsourcing many state services, and by 2007, 20 per cent of UK public expenditure was on outsourced services.[51] As these were privatized, many were floated on the London Stock Exchange, effectively embroiling great swathes of UK public services to London's financial sector. While private shareholders benefit, profits are made by squeezing workers, who, unlike their publicly employed colleagues, don't benefit from decades of public sector union negotiations and therefore have lower pay, worse conditions and fewer routes for progression.[52] For example, cleaners, porters and catering staff at St Mary's Hospital in London, who were outsourced through global company Sodexo, had pay and conditions substantially worse than colleagues employed directly by the NHS. During a campaign and strike, one of their unions, United Voices of the World, identified multiple cases of mismanagement and poor treatment, saying that 'as a union we have never seen such a large quantity of cases of such severe nature on any one contract'.[53]

Under financial capitalism, the odds are against workers, whether organized or not. In an attempt to enthuse a struggling labour movement, union advocates declare that 'if workers refuse to work, the bosses can't produce anything . . . that's the power of a strike'.[54] And yet for workers at Tops Markets, Carillion or GE, it doesn't always feel like that. Far from being the main cog in a profit-making machine, workers increasingly find themselves side-lined by company owners who have worked out increasingly effective ways to make money while being much less beholden to workers on the ground. Workers in the private sector are most directly affected. But with increased outsourcing and the financialization of the public sector, no workers are immune.

Wealth out of the reach of workers

The financialization of firms has redirected money away from workers and towards directors and shareholders. But even if workers were able to tackle these issues firm by firm, they would still be losing out overall. That's because *at an economy-wide level*, capital is flowing towards rent-seeking (rather than productive) sectors.

One of the most insightful studies on these dynamics comes from within the labour movement itself. After two decades organizing in workplace struggles in the US and Europe, union researcher John Burant was struck by how hard it was for unions to make any serious headway in reducing overall economic inequality. To understand what was going on, he zoomed out and asked where the big profits are actually being generated in the US economy. His study had a simple finding: while *workers* are concentrated in sectors that generate little aggregate profit, such as retail, care and education, *profits* are concentrated in sectors with relatively few employees.[55] This trend has increased dramatically over recent decades. Top of the list of sectors with high profits are, unsurprisingly, finance and real estate (property and housing). This creates what Burant calls a 'sectoral trap'. Unions, by virtue of the fact they are organizations of workers, operate in sectors where workers are, but these are the sectors which lay claim to the least substantial portion of profits.

High levels of self-employment in the UK make calculating this trend more complicated, but the data available suggests a similar picture. As a rule, sectors with relatively low rates of employment, such as finance and insurance, have high and increasing profit margins, while those with high rates of employment, such as transportation, hotels and restaurants, have low and decreasing profit margins.[56]

At the centre of this story is the massive increase in the size and profitability of the financial sector. Between 1997 and 2010, the increase in the share of financial and insurance services in the UK economy was greater than the increase in the share of any other sector apart from government.[57] More recently, while overall economic growth has been sluggish, the growth that has occurred has been led by business services and finance.[58]

This increase in the size and profitability of the finance sector has been a major cause of increased economic inequality. It has been one of the main causes of the decline in the labour share, and even within that share, huge increases in income for top earners in the finance sector have left even less for the other 99 per cent.[59]

The 'sectoral trap' has profound implications for labour movement strategy. Unions can certainly increase wages by organizing in high-employment, low-profit sectors, and these gains would create real improvements in people's lives now. But there will be a limit to the extent to which this work can stem overall inequalities of money and power. Even if unions were successful in achieving a minimum wage of $15 an hour (a current goal for US unions), the reduction in overall inequality would be less substantial than we might think, because so much of the increase in inequality is due to ballooning wealth at the top. It would amount, Burant argues, to at most 'a minor challenge to the status of the 1%.'[60] If the fundamental aim of the labour movement is to redistribute power towards workers, rather than just increase wages, then its current organizing model isn't hitting capital where it hurts.

Finance profiting from workers in other ways

Not only is finance undermining union power for workers in the US and UK, but it is also exploiting them more intensively in other ways. It's not that the rich no longer rely on workers for their wealth: they do. Rather, what has changed is that methods of extracting that wealth are shifting. While capitalism has always been based on capital owners profiting from the labour of workers, the owners increasingly also do so through extracting economic rent from those same workers – through high housing rents, interest payments on debt, insurance products to cover the absence of benefits and protections, and extracting taxes through financialized public services.

Personal debt plays a particularly important role. The level of debt that people are driven to take on in order to pay their rent, buy groceries or cover education or healthcare costs has ballooned, particularly since the early 2000s. Despite a short dip after the financial crisis, debt levels in the US and the UK are now both higher than their pre-2008 peak.[61] Debt repayments are one of the most directly regressive elements of modern economies, providing a mechanism by which money is syphoned from the poor to the rich. In the UK, 90 per cent of households were contributors to banks. Only the 10 per cent of households with the highest incomes were net beneficiaries of interest paid by the rest.[62]

This papering over the cracks in household finances by borrowing has come to be known as 'debtfare'.[63]

Susanne Soederberg argues that debt is critical to the proliferation of poor employment practices and work insecurity because people who are stuck paying back high-interest loans feel they have to take work even if it is low-paid and insecure. People may be deterred from taking industrial action, particularly long-term action that results in sustained loss of wages.[64] Such debtors are further exploited by (and provide ample demand for) payday loans, pawn shops and expensive credit. This exploitation was laid bare recently, in a 'rare attack of honesty', by payday lenders in Arizona who explained they were opposing minimum wage legislation because if people had enough money, they wouldn't need short-term loans.[65]

In a parallel process, a heavily financialized housing system has increased both rents and house prices to an incredibly high level. As house prices are determined more by the role of property as a financial asset than by people's demand for places to live, housing costs have been increasing much faster than wages.[66]

In this way, personal debt and high housing costs benefit capital twice over: firstly directly through interest payments and rent, and secondly by keeping workers financially insecure, weakening their power in the workplace.

Even within the workplace, financialization has found new ways to make money from workers through financial means. Take Uber as an example. Uber's entire business model relies on miscategorizing their drivers as 'self-employed' workers, shifting risk from the employer to the worker. Unionized drivers on both sides of the Atlantic have recently been making headlines, objecting to this exploitation, including financial exploitation.

Models like Uber that are reliant on deregulated labour also rely on deregulated capital. Drivers can only work if they can buy their own car and insurance, which many can't afford – 33 per cent of drivers in the District of Columbia, for example, had to take out loans.[67] Uber itself has spotted the potential for profit, and now provides insurance and loan services directly, negotiating bulk discounts, selling them on to drivers at a higher cost and pocketing the difference.[68] As financial commentator Izabella Kaminska points out, 'It's literally the equivalent of a company you work for selling you the equipment you need to do your job at a rate that far exceeds their sourcing cost (because they were able to negotiate in bulk on your collective behalf while you could not).'[69]

Under political pressure from a UK legal case, won in 2016, which ruled that Uber drivers should be counted as workers, and which Uber is appealing, the company has set up a deal with AXA Insurance to provide loss-of-earnings payments for drivers who are sick or need time off for parental duties.[70] However, this also means that organized drivers would have to face an insurance firm, and not their de facto employer, to bargain for better terms or settle disputes. Even basic employment rights like sick pay, it seems, are becoming financialized.

Just like the case of corporations using 'dead peasants insurance' to offset their labour costs, these examples demonstrate how, under financialization, company owners treat workers as another asset to speculate on. The owners profit from their workers' labour and also profit indirectly, by creating a captive market (their workforce) whose needs they control and whom they can sell services to, or take out financial products on behalf of.

One of the implications of the centrality of rent-seeking in our economies is the increasing importance of wealth over income in determining one's life chances. Even a household with two earners on reasonable salaries is no longer able to save enough for a deposit to purchase a home in many areas of the UK and US. Whether or not you can get on the 'housing ladder' often depends more on family wealth (often inherited) than on earned income. In the UK, the average contribution from living parents is now a staggering £24,100,[71] and those without access to a 'bank of mum and dad' are stuck paying soaring rents to enriched landlords, entrenching inequality between families over generations.

By making it easier to make money from having money, financialization exacerbates wealth inequality. In the US, average household wealth increased from 250 per cent of income in 1970 to 400 per cent in 2015.[72] The new wealth was not accumulated by traditional savings. In fact, savings rates have generally decreased since the 1970s. Rather, it was accumulated through capital gains in the stock and housing markets. Meanwhile in the UK, one in five baby boomers are millionaires, mostly through increases in house prices.[73]

At the same time, those without the savings to get them through unexpected events, such as a broken car or a family funeral, are more likely to end up in spiralling personal debt. While the lottery of birth has always determined much of people's life chances under capitalism, financialization inflates its importance. This is reflected in the substantial decline in 'social mobility' in the UK in the second half of the twentieth-century.[74] While much is made of high income inequality in the US and the UK, wealth inequality is in fact much more extreme, and has been increasing more quickly in recent decades.[75]

Finance undermines democracy

Financialization has also fuelled a level of economic inequality that undermines the democratic functioning of society. Under globalized financial capitalism, the finance sector and wealthy company owners hold massive sway over national policy making. By threatening 'capital strikes' or 'capital flights' – in other words, taking their money and leaving – they wield serious power.

Given the damage they do, would this matter? The problem is that, in the US and the UK, financial activity not only leads economic growth but is also a major export. This matters because we buy a lot more from other countries than we sell to them. This is a major economic weakness and any reduction in financial exports would weaken our economies still further. These dynamics are especially acute in the UK, where financial services make up a particularly large portion of exports.

Furthermore, although there is a deficit in our trade, national accounts still have to balance. This means we essentially borrow the shortfall from international financiers in the form of 'foreign direct investment' to the US and UK, making us reliant on financiers to balance up.[76]

This would put any government serious about curbing the power of finance in a major bind. Transitioning away from financialization cannot be done overnight and a sudden exodus of domestic and foreign finance capital, deliberately delivered as a political punishment, would be a substantial threat to economic stability. And it's not an empty threat – capital flight has played a role in bringing down radical left governments, such as Syriza in Greece.[77]

Like hostages suffering Stockholm syndrome, we find ourselves beholden to finance just as it denies us freedom and independence.

Globalization, deindustrialization and the shift to service sectors

Financialization has gone hand in hand with globalization and deindustrialization. These trends have been mutually reinforcing: as globalization made it less profitable to manufacture goods domestically, capital was directed more towards rent-seeking than domestic manufacturing, and, starved of investment, the British and American industrial base weakened still further. These trends have occurred at the firm level, but also on an economy-wide level – one indicator of which is the significant reduction in the amount of bank credit going to non-financial firms since the 1990s.[78]

However, while manufacturing has declined (employing 5.7 million workers in 1981 in the UK compared to just 2.7 million in 2018),[79] this has been compensated for by an increase in the service sector, which has ballooned in the US and the UK, propping up employment rates.

In many ways, workers in the service sector are less directly affected by financialization than those in manufacturing jobs, and it's no surprise that, particularly in the US, some of the most exciting union activity has been taking place in often woman-dominated service industries.[80] However, the problem is that this service sector is dominated on the one hand by finance and business services – generally highly paid workers who are unlikely to become agitators against their own sectors – and on the other by low-paid industries such as care and retail. Some of these latter roles have a somewhat reduced bargaining power anyway because workers are considered low-skilled and, in our jobs market, therefore easy to replace. As we go on to discuss in later chapters, these are important areas for unions to focus on, particularly as they are often dominated by female workers, immigrants and people of colour who face multiple oppressions. But they are also industries with small profit margins, so that even when union wins are able to get a better deal for workers, there's a limit to how much.

All this raises yet another question. If financial capitalism is so bad at making things in the real economy, how come we all have so much stuff? The answer, of course, is that it's being produced in other countries, often in much worse labour conditions than those in the US and UK. This has happened through a combination of offshoring and international trade, but one way or another, much of the profit from this labour exploitation flows back to transnational corporations headquartered in wealthy nations.[81] This labour exploitation is increasingly being resisted by large movements of organized labour, with mass recruitment and strikes across industrializing countries such as South Korea, Nigeria, South Africa and Brazil since the mid-1990s.[82]

Change is coming

Understanding how financialization weakens workers and unions is the easy bit. Working out what to do about it is much harder. Today's unions – built for industrial capitalism – are currently struggling to cut through in a finance-driven economy.The only way to tackle financialization is for unions themselves to get ahead of the curve – to proactively help to build a new economy as well as resisting the injustices of the existing one. This is the topic of the next three chapters.

However, as unions develop strategies to tackle financial capitalism, they must do so in a way that takes into account the interconnected challenges of climate change and slowing global growth. A swelling international movement of climate strikers and protesters, backed by a number of unions, has pushed climate change up the political agenda and is setting a new course for militant action against the governments and business sponsoring the fossil-fuel economy. Climate change requires a scale of mobilization that neither the UK nor US has before seen in peace time, or perhaps ever.

Coming to terms with ecological crisis – both the tangible impacts of fires, floods and droughts, and the work needed to decarbonize and undertake massive habitat restoration – will be a defining issue facing unions in the coming decades. So far, the response has been fraught with tension. The aim of protecting the jobs of workers in carbon-heavy industries like fossil fuel and air transport has been put at odds with the broader interests of workers across the globe, and in particular the Global South, who will undoubtedly suffer the most if rapid solutions to the crisis are not found.

Unions are also likely to have another set of dynamics to reckon with – the limits of economic growth. Climate change is largely the result of ballooning consumption and growth in the Global North, and there is so far little evidence that such growth can continue alongside an absolute reduction in carbon emissions and reversing ecological degradation.[83] With an economic model reliant on growth, it's unlikely that political leaders will take the leap to deliberately pursue a low or no-growth economy as part of a green transition plan. But, whether planned for or not, growth has significantly slowed across advanced capitalist countries since the financial crash, and there are limited prospects for its return.

Worryingly, political economist Beth Stratford has argued that low levels of growth are likely to result in an intensity of the kinds of rent-seeking we've discussed above.[84] Financial elites are used to high returns on their investments, but this can only happen consistently in an economy that's growing. The closer we get to zero growth, the closer we get to a zero-sum game when it comes to consumption. If production and consumption stop growing, then when some people consume more, other people have to consume less. If owners of capital can't increase their wealth by making and consuming more stuff, attention will turn even more towards making claims over the spoils from *existing* production and assets.

In practice, this might mean more land- and resource-grabbing, aggressive use of intellectual property and monopoly powers to block competition, and pressure to privatize public and common infrastructures. Those who already have access to assets are likely to intensify their rent-seeking, unless they are stopped.

2

Understanding and rebuilding union power

On 12 December 2019 Britain voted for another five years of Conservative rule, with one of Labour's most crushing defeats of a generation. The Labour vote across the 'red wall' – a strip of post-industrial constituencies in the North of England – finally crumbled, after years of decline. Following the defeat, Twitter was awash with shrill recriminations, with commentators blaming the party's Brexit strategy, the leader's style or a biased press. But beyond the hot takes, a deeper lesson is emerging, one that requires looking back not weeks or months, but decades. The recent defeat of the Labour Party must be understood in the context of a longer defeat of organized labour as a presence in workplaces, communities and politics.

Across the 'red wall', as well as in many other parts of the UK and the US, the mines, manufacturing plants and shipbuilding yards that once anchored the local economies have closed. Public services like hospitals, buses and schools have faced crippling funding cuts, privatization and closure. Successive Conservative *and Labour* governments have robbed many communities of their identity and purpose, replacing them with Amazon warehouses, call centres, precarious contracts and distant bosses.

With the loss of these industries, many of the cultures and institutions of the labour movement have also been lost. Self-organized mutual aid and working men's clubs, local newspapers and, crucially, trade unions have withdrawn, died or dwindled to irrelevance. Meanwhile many migrants and working-class people of colour, who have been either ignored or aggressively excluded from these institutions, have watched the Labour Party fuel anti-Muslim sentiment in the wake of 9/11 and, along with some union leaders, back anti-immigration policies since.

In the US, too, hopes for a democratic socialist revival will have to wait at least another term. Bernie Sanders, now out of the running, campaigned with an economic programme similar to that of the UK Labour Party under Jeremy Corbyn, with labour and union rights centre stage. The programme promised to involve unions in the setting of minimum standards across whole industries, not just employer by employer.[1] Akin to models in operation in many European countries, 'sectoral collective bargaining', which agrees terms and conditions across a whole sector supported by legislation, would have marked a huge new power for unions.

Labour's plans – now shelved as the party endures five years in opposition – also detailed a model for rebuilding union power via legislative means. Plans proposed new 'Sectoral Employment Commissions' and wage councils which would set minimum terms for workers across whole industries, prioritizing care and gig economy sectors where union membership is low and precarious working conditions are rife.[2] As the COVID-19 pandemic unfolds, these shelved policies represent a huge missed opportunity to show respect for and shore up the livelihoods of the most precarious workers on whom economies rely. It is shameful that it has taken such grave circumstances to force governments to recognize the huge economic and societal contribution these workers make. The overnight appreciation of the role of carers, supermarket cashiers, refuse workers, drivers and couriers by governments under Boris Johnson and Donald Trump should not be misrecognized as an ideological shift. Until those in power act to radically improve the material conditions of those workers, their rhetorical appreciation has little weight.

Labour's proposals to boost not just the material conditions of these workers, but also their voice and power, through sectoral collective bargaining were designed with the Trades Union Congress (TUC, the national union confederation), with widespread support from the union movement. With diminishing membership and industrial strength, they couldn't afford to ignore such chances. But most knew that these reforms were not just a long shot politically, but if won, would mark the start of a battle, not the end.

The challenge: empowering unions to be a force against finance

The transatlantic revival of support for an institutional role for unions in shaping the economy is significant. It formed a key part of emergent political projects that sought to replace neoliberalism – the dogma that has enabled organized finance to rule – with a system that puts democracy at the centre of economic planning.

This is a much bigger ambition than regulating finance alone. Since the financial crash, progressive policy wonks and economists have called for tighter financial regulation, but with little progress so far. There is no shortage of good ideas – including introducing taxes to slow down financial activity or reduce its profitability, preventing finance from moving across national borders, or waging war on tax avoidance. What's lacking is the power to usher them in. While these policies would temper finance and rebalance the economy in favour of labour, they will remain on the shelf unless a movement is built that can elect and defend a government willing to make them happen.

Even with a genuinely progressive political party in power – and this is the crux – waging a policy war on finance and promoting a greater role for unions will be incredibly hard. Any government serious about curbing the power of major capital owners can expect a strong counter-attack, including coordinated capital strikes and an entrenched network of revolving doors as people move between politics, government and the private sector, ready to scupper reforms at every turn.[3] Regulation that reduces the power of elites is only as powerful as the movement that can defend and maintain it.

Unions are essential to the type of strong, genuinely *democratic* socialism that is capable of tempering finance in this way. As we are learning in the UK, they are a precondition for this type of political party to secure and maintain power in government. But this presents a conundrum: as governments which are actively hostile to unions settle down for more years in office, how can the movement rebuild enough strength to usher in something new?

What is union power?

> We always focus on what's the percentage of people in unions, and what the percentage of coverage is – without really thinking about where our power lies and who our target is. Which employers, which industries? Where do we have power and where do we need to build it?
>
> Andrew Towers, head of political strategy, Communication Workers Union[4]

It's worth pausing to talk about what we mean by union power. To be an effective vehicle for the pursuit of economic and political change, unions need to build and exercise collective power. Their ability to do so effectively is based on a number of conditions. This includes organizational capacity – whether a union is able to build the fundamental relationships and identify leaders that enable them to mobilize a large enough base of people to take effective collective action.[5] For this, leadership, organizing strategy and resources matter, and these can be thought of as some of the major 'internal' conditions that determine a union's ability to exercise power. Without organizational power, all other powers are fairly meaningless.

But other conditions are also crucial in determining the success of union actions. 'Discursive power' is the extent to which workers are able to produce collective identities, legitimate their claims morally and symbolically, and challenge dominant narratives. It is crucial both for building solidarity internally, promoting sufficient militancy among the membership to take action, and for winning the arguments externally.[6]

Structural power is the objective, material power of workers.[7] The critical structural power that underpins unions is that of withdrawing labour – going on strike – and it is a right that has been hard won in capitalist economies. Under a wage-capital system, withholding your labour is arguably the only mechanism outside of statutory regulation by which employers can be held to account. It is the fundamental act of economic disruption by workers, and where it is properly enshrined as a right, it functions as a potential as much as it does an action.

Facilitating strike action, or at least enabling its potential, is the foundation of 'industrial unionism', which recognizes the collective labour of workers as the primary source of profit-making in a company or industry.[8] This is in contrast to 'craft unions', which base their structural power on maintaining standards across a particular skill, and preventing undercutting by cheaper competitors by negotiating collectively over the rates of pay for their products.[9] Most unions today include a combination of these traditions.

In the previous chapter we discussed how financialization is undermining the organizing and structural power of unions. As debt-fuelled companies race each other to the bottom on worker's rights, and capital owners amass huge amounts of wealth in ways that sidestep labour, the potential for economic disruption workers collectively wield is dampened and opportunities to deploy it are reduced.

But other forms of union power have also been

undermined during the past forty years of neoliberalism. The values of individualism and private interests have won out over those of welfare in economic decision-making. We're in an age of insurance, landlordism and personal debt, chipping away at the discursive power of trade unionism, based on solidarity and collective aid.

Last, there is institutional power – the extent to which labour law and institutions are on the side of workers, including the incorporation of past collective wins into economic programmes and deals made between unions and the state. One celebrated example of this is the establishment of the British welfare state, which was consolidated by the political wing of the unions, the Labour Party, and plays a continued role in supporting workers to have a basic level of economic security, underpinning their structural power in the economy. Today, the recent popular surge around democratic socialist movements in the US and the UK has prised open a discussion on the role of public policy in rebuilding the institutional power of unions.

In the following sections we look at how the institutional power of UK and US unions over the last forty years has been eroded, and how this changes the landscape for union renewal. We ask what the progressive political projects of today can learn from the past – as well as from continental Europe, where unions have been particularly embedded in institutional decision-making, both historically and today.

Looking back: the rise and decline of union power

Industrial unions were built in the late nineteenth century and the early twentieth century across Europe and the US under the explosion of the factory system.[10] Their bargaining strength was based on their capacity to unite different groups of workers within the same company, sector or location, underpinned by the material power to go on strike.[11] Responding to the vast growth in the scale of industry and the formation of new cities, these unions became mass membership bodies including women, unskilled and semi-skilled workers.[12]

A defining moment in this history was the growth of 'new' unions in Britain between 1888 and 1892, which built power and membership through mass strikes, doubling union membership in just a few years.[13] Unlike craft unions, which relied for their power on the *scarcity* of labour, these unions drew their strength from numbers,[14] with tactics including mass meetings, workplace stewards, community agitation and street stalls. They adopted broad socialist goals, aiming to assert the interests of labour as a class, against exploitation by the elites.[15]

In the US, the traditions of craft unionism had never been as strong. Just as in the UK, the large increase in demand for manual labourers to operate machinery at the end of the nineteenth century saw union membership among unskilled workers soar.[16] Large industrial unions of these growing workforces emerged, which confederated across the country.[17]

The 'golden age' of union power

In the first half of the twentieth century, the union movements on both sides of the Atlantic amassed great political and industrial power. Their strength during this period was both the result – and also part of the cause – of the social democratic consensus that came to characterize the era, when a new type of collaboration between labour, capital and the state emerged.[18]

In the US, the New Deals of the 1930s, developed in response to the Great Depression, had brought tremendous gains for labour, with major pieces of legislation requiring businesses to bargain in good faith with unions.[19] In the UK, as part of the 'post-war compromise' following the Second World War, governments nationalized key industries, introduced a generous welfare state and passed legislation that protected workers, whilst reigning in finance. Employer practice was regulated through wage councils, which involved union representatives, and a raft of sectoral union agreements.[20]

As the economies and business confidence grew, employers began to respond to union demands with higher wages and better working conditions. Supported by sectoral bargaining agreements, pay rates tended to become consistent within a sector and so not an area of competition between employers, who therefore had time and resources to focus on other elements of their operations.[21]

The results by the 1950s and 1960s were dramatic. The period saw unprecedented levels of economic growth on both sides of the Atlantic, relatively low economic inequality (though deep gender and racial inequalities remained), low unemployment, decreasing working hours and a steadily growing labour share.[22] By the late 1970s half the UK working population were in unions and over 80 per cent were covered by collective agreements. At this time in the US 20 per cent of workers were unionized, following a peak in the 1950s.[23]

Growth was partly enabled by the prevalent Fordist regime of the era, which produced large, hierarchically organized firms in which unions thrived.[24] The development of mass production based on task fragmentation, known as 'Taylorism', brought about tremendous gains in productivity, which enabled the real incomes of workers to rise and working hours to decline, while capital owners also saw large increases in profits. Not only did Fordism involve a major reordering of production techniques, it also saw the birth of a new type of relationship between bosses and workers, with increased managerial control of workplace practices. In this new model it became common for union officials to play a central and formalized role in setting standards in agreement with employers.[25]

Unions during this period had both government support and high levels of membership, providing a major bulwark against the unlimited prerogatives of business. Union leaders built their reputations on the security that this institutional power offered to workers: rising wages and policies that promised reliable, continuous employment.[26] This often came at the cost of broader working-class aims of equal pay, racial justice, and the expansion of the union movement at large beyond white, male, industrial sectors.[27]

However, this institutional power was not to last.

The attack on unions

The 1980s ushered in a new climate for unions. When the post-war economic consensus faltered with a series of global economic shocks throughout the 1970s, a new, neoliberal economic ideology was waiting in the wings. Just as neoliberalism set capital free through financialization, it simultaneously reduced the power of labour through a dramatic overhaul of labour market regulations. Despite claiming an ideological commitment to deregulation, neoliberal governments in the US and UK created a host of new and complex regulations for unions.

The UK's legislative attack started in 1979 under Thatcher and continued through no fewer than ten major legislative acts aimed at fragmenting and, ultimately, criminalizing some union activities. There were two main thrusts to the anti-union agenda. Firstly, legislation chipped away at the ability of strikers to mobilize community solidarity.[28] During the closure of many coal mines in the 1980s, miners successfully mobilized mass, community pickets to great effect. Thatcher directly attacked this strategy, outlawing the participation of non-strikers, whether local residents, family members or workers from neighbouring workplaces, from showing solidarity on picket lines. Secondly, sectoral bargaining structures, which had given unions a formal role in negotiating wages for an entire sector, were broken up. This destabilized unions' role in setting conditions and wages, compounded by parallel labour market liberalization that enabled new forms of more casualized working practices to emerge.

A crucial aim of this regulatory change was to limit

the role of unions to the workplace. Union efforts to build a social role beyond narrow pay disputes were quashed by new legal constraints put on union campaigning. Only workers directly affected by changes to their conditions were allowed to contest that change – a move towards the conception of union membership as a workplace insurance policy rather than a social and political project. This was consolidated in the late 1990s when New Labour introduced 'right to representation' legislation, which had the effect of prioritizing the rights of individual workers to access one-to-one union representation, as part of case work and disputes, over other union activities such as recruiting, campaigning and collective bargaining.[29]

By the end of the twentieth century a shallow-rooted form of bargaining had emerged as a result, with an approach of 'workplace partnership' between unions and management replacing the more confrontational methods that went before.[30] Parts of the union movement have been complicit in this de-politicization of a union's role. As Becki Winson, a UK organizer, explains:

> Large chunks of the union bureaucracy at the time happily went along with it, and many still do. There doesn't need to be a trade-off between helping individual members and taking collective action. There's nothing to stop reps bringing individual cases to mass meetings and calling for industrial action based on them. Unions just haven't been encouraging their members and shop stewards to do it.[31]

As well as facing legislative attacks, unions also faced renewed attacks from industry itself. In the US, emboldened by the anti-worker and pro-business sentiment of the Reagan administration, a whole industry bloomed around strike and union busting that still operates today. As one specialist in union oppression, writing in the *Wall Street Journal* in 1984, explained: 'the current [Reagan] government and business climate presents a unique opportunity for companies . . . to develop and implement long-term plans for conducting business in a union-free environment'.[32]

Starting with a few consultants offering businesses advice in 'union avoidance' in the 1950s, this industry boomed in the late 1970s and 1980s and amassed a turnover of hundreds of millions of dollars each year.[33] Later, employers began to demand more subtle and sophisticated tactics and the field of 'preventive labour relations' was born. Professionals in the field wielded degrees in industrial psychology, management and labour law – with skills to manipulate not only the provisions of labour law, but also the emotions of workers seeking to unionize.[34] These practices existed, albeit more covertly, in the UK too. Despite 'blacklisting' being outlawed in 1999, a legal case settled in 2019 found that more than forty major construction firms funded and maintained confidential files on 3,200 workers between 1993 and 2009, pooling information about their employment histories, political views and personal relationships and using it to shut unionized workers out of the industry.[35]

This long period of retrenchment, which endures today under the Johnson and Trump administrations, continues the aim of keeping unions in a box. Both legislation and the union-avoidance industry have conspired to confine unions to narrow workplace disputes, with strict rules and new cultural norms that limit which fights they pick and the tactics they use. These tactics seem to have been at least in part effective. In the post-war years between 1945 and 1979, days lost to strikes in the UK averaged 5.9 million per year. Between 1990 and 2018 they averaged 0.8 million per year, and not once reached 2 million.[36]

The demise of collective bargaining

One of the functions that has been gradually eroded during this period is the role of unions in collective bargaining over pay and conditions. During the post-war period unions were an institutionalized force in the economy, to the extent that, by the late 1970s, most British workers had their wages set via some sort of collective agreement involving unions.[37] Today it's roughly a quarter.[38] In the US, the high point came in the 1950s when a third of the workforce were in unions and had their wages set via a union. Today it is one in ten.

Weak union coverage and the dramatically reduced involvement of unions in pay setting are a deliberate outcome of the neoliberal agenda. In the UK, this took the form of undoing the sectoral bargaining agreements that had determined working conditions across whole industries. Labour market deregulation in the UK was ushered in through the Wages Act of 1986 and subsequent reforms in the early 1990s that dismantled the UK's wage councils – the associations of employers and employee representatives who would set wages and standards across industries.

The result is that pay setting has been effectively taken 'in house' by firms. The privatization of major industries speeded up this process, as new and changed workplaces increasingly fell outside the reach of existing bargaining agreements. Though collective bargaining has remained strong in some privatized industries where natural monopolies exist, such as transport and energy,[39] in other parts of the private sector entirely un-unionized workplaces have proliferated.

As a result of the closure of the wage councils and demise of sector-wide agreements, for a period in the early 1990s the UK was the only country in the European Community to have no statutory or implicit means to ensure minimum standards of pay.[40] The introduction of the National Minimum Wage under Blair in 1999 sought to address this, ameliorating the conditions of the worst-off through unilateral, statutory means and deliberately avoiding the re-establishment of collective bargaining or wage boards.[41]

In the US, collective bargaining has always been decentralized, operating at an enterprise-by-enterprise level, and so the institutional power of unions did not have so far to fall.[42] But a major blow came in 1947 with a new piece of legislation known as the 'Taft–Hartley Act', which allowed individual states to enact 'right to work' laws and opt out of certain collective bargaining regulations.[43] Half of all US states have now adopted these rules, mostly in the South and Mid-West, with workers in some 'right to work states' earning 8 per cent less per hour than their counterparts in neighbouring states.[44]

This fragmentation is exacerbated further by the fact that the rights of workers to bargain collectively differ not just from state to state, but depending on which industries they work in. There are three distinct legal regimes: one for the railroad and airline industries, one for the rest of the private sector, and one for the public sector.[45] In the public sector, which has much higher union density, the rules are especially restrictive, with striking and other industrial action prohibited for many.[46]

The demise of collective bargaining means that, for most US and UK workers today, voting for a party that promises to increase the minimum wage is the closest they get to having a say in their terms of employment. Under Anglophone common-law regimes the absence of collective bargaining means 'the employment contract provides the employer with a licence to command'.[47]

Going against the grain, some US states have recently begun coordinating a form of collective bargaining for low-paid workers at a local level. California, New York and New Jersey are among a number of US states to have passed laws to establish wage boards that include management, public officials and representatives of the workforce in setting standards in certain industries.[48] In 2015 the New York state wage board was one of the first districts to authorize a $15 hourly minimum wage for fast-food workers in businesses that are part of chains, phased in over six years.[49] The corresponding 'Fight for Fifteen' campaign that spread across the country involving young McDonald's workers rolled this out to seven more states.[50]

The state of play today: organizing without institutional power

> We're having to basically start from scratch. As a union movement I'm not sure we're ready for the scale of recruitment and organizing that's needed.
>
> UK union organizer[51]

Since the 1980s, unions have struggled to rebuild power. They are failing to reach many workers in new industries, partly because of economic changes such as financialization which make their work harder, but also because of limitations in the movement's own structures and cultures.

In the absence of sector-wide bargaining, the main way to increase the coverage of collective bargaining is to increase the number of unionized workplaces, which requires building new membership bases in areas of the economy where there isn't one. And this is not easy. Over the past forty years, unions have made few serious inroads into the growing private sector industries in which the majority of the population work – from distribution warehouses to private care homes, supermarkets, hotels and call centres. Private sector union membership on both sides of the Atlantic declined sharply in the final two decades of the twentieth century and has continued in a downward trajectory, albeit more slowly, since. In 2018 only 13.2 per cent of UK private sector workers were in a union, and only 6.4 per cent in the US. The case in the hospitality sector is particularly stark – only around 3 per cent of British and US hospitality workers are in a union.[52]

Because private sector membership is so low, an increasing portion of the population has no access to – or even knowledge of – unions. This creates a self-reinforcing cycle of decline and compounds low membership among young workers. In the UK, membership among 18–25-year-olds has halved since the millennium.[53]

There are important exceptions to this rule. In the US there has been a notable recent increase in young members in both the private and public sectors – in 2017 this meant that one in four new jobs taken up by under-35s was unionized.[54] New branches are being established in the US, including in tech start-ups, among game-workers and in the warehouses of online retailers. In the UK, campaigns by bartenders, cinema staff, fast-food workers and gig economy couriers have taken place in major cities, many led by young and migrant workers.

But in these industries without a strong union legacy, there are only a handful of instances in which a sufficient density of union membership has been built to take industrial action and win improved conditions. There is good reason for this. Face-to-face workplace organizing today is hard. Work is increasingly physically fragmented with workforces often spread over several sites. Insecure and shift-based jobs lead to a higher staff turnover and anonymous workplace cultures.[55] Unions are often unable to physically access workers, either because they are within locked buildings or because they are subject to surveillance or threats from anti-union management.[56] While these conditions make union organizing a challenge, they are not insurmountable. But they do mean that organizing in new industries tends to be resource intensive, and because income from membership is shrinking, unions are risk averse about spending. As one UK union organizer put it:

> We're not even close to being fit for purpose to recruit, and part of the problem is to do with our own structures. Our time is always torn between servicing existing members here and recruiting hypothetical future members over there.[57]

Established unions often remain disproportionately focused on 'legacy' industries such as utilities, rail, buses and post – industries which used to be in public ownership and where union density was historically and is currently higher than average. Most private sector membership today is in fact concentrated in these industries, as they have shifted from the public to the private sectors. While unions prioritize their resources for representing these existing members and maintaining current recognition agreements, ambitions to organize for more political, outward-looking campaigns lose out. Many union recruitment strategies today are explicitly focused on 'infill' (aiming to improve density where there is already a union active), rather than expanding into new sectors.[58]

This failure has serious consequences beyond dwindling membership. Migrant, black and other workers from ethnic minorities face exclusion from the union movement as they are more likely to work in the types of insecure, private sector jobs that unions struggle to organize, and even within unionized workplaces they face difficulties ensuring effective representation of their interests.[59]

The prioritization of legacy members at the cost of reaching beyond is reminiscent of a 'craft union' approach focused on 'looking after your own'. In some cases this is an intentional strategy: defend existing working standards *against* the introduction of the poorer standards (and by implication new workers) that undermine them.[60] As one organizer puts it:

> There are political and strategic issues to think through. Should we go and recruit people in new companies that have resulted from a liberalisation of the market, if we don't think these companies should exist at all?[61]

But while workers in new, privatized industries are suffering some of the worst conditions, the union movement's failure to build joint strategies across sectors is a failure to build real working-class solidarity.

The massive outsourcing of public services such as hospitals, prisons and universities in the UK is one example of this failure, and something many unions have been slow to adapt to. The two- and three-tier workforces created by outsourcing are often mirrored by unions themselves. It is not unusual for one union to represent certain professional groups that have remained 'in house' to a service, such as technicians in a university or clerks in a hospital, with another organizing among the outsourced cleaners and caterers who don't have parity of pay, job security or rights. And these unions don't always work together. There are perceived trade-offs for established unions who are defending the rights of their long-standing in-house members. Indeed, picking a fight over the poor standards of outsourced workers might mean putting long-standing bargaining agreements covering in-house members at risk.

Newer, independent unions in the UK such as Independent Workers Union of Great Britain (IWGB) and United Voices of the World (UVW) have been vocal on this issue, accusing the broader union movement of protectionism. They have made it their business to take up cases that they feel the bigger unions are failing on, such as the recent case won by 1,000 outsourced hospital workers – cleaners, porters and security staff – most of whom are migrants from Europe, Africa, Latin America and Asia, to be insourced in a London hospital.[62] In theory, sectoral bargaining could overcome these divisions between different groups of workers by raising everyone's wages together. However, even if a government were to introduce this, substantial work would still remain, both to ensure that these powers are democratic and accountable to the workforce they seek to serve, and to make them resilient to political change. Both of these things, as we can see from the live case unfolding in France, are never a given.

Lessons from Europe

At midday on 22 September 2017, in a carefully staged and televised ceremony, French president Emmanuel Macron signed five decrees dramatically weakening France's labour laws. The former investment banker proudly hailed them as 'without precedent' in the post-war French Fifth Republic.

The reforms constituted a major deregulation of the labour market, including undermining France's system of sectoral bargaining. That system had meant that up to then, 98 per cent of France's population was covered by collective bargaining, despite only 8 per cent actually being members of a union (and most of these, as in the US and UK, consigned to the public sector).[63] Macron's reforms allowed individual firms to come to their own agreements, undermining those conditions negotiated at a higher level.

Labour reform had been a key plank of Macron's pro-business, pro-finance presidential campaign and was controversially pushed through by executive order during the first months of his presidency. But labour law reform in France is not for the faint-hearted. Four presidents over the last thirty years have attempted it and been met with profound public resistance.[64] Macron too has met considerable resistance from French unions, who are demonstrating that even under hostile governments and with low membership, unions can still flex their muscles, with some success.

National strikes over proposals to increase the pensionable age have erupted. This follows the steady building of grassroots activity focused largely on France's public transport networks,[65] with recent direct action by private sector unions – such as energy workers – cutting off power supplies across the suburbs south of Paris.

These efforts, however, have not managed to prevent one of the key pieces of legislative infrastructure that gives unions a formalized role in the economy – sectoral bargaining – from being diluted. And this spells trouble for a movement with so few paid-up members. In the context of a hostile government, it remains to be seen how much French unions can maintain their impressive militancy, capacity to mobilize and institutional role.

Unions still play important institutional roles in state agendas across Europe today, but this role is in retreat, to differing degrees, almost everywhere.[66] Sometimes referred to as forms of 'social dialogue', 'social partnerships', 'tripartite agreements' or 'corporatism', institutional unionism represents attempts to *formalize* the role of unions in workplaces, in sectors of the economy and in relation to the state. It is no secret that institutional unionism in the US and UK lags well behind that of Europe. Today the UK is an outlier among its neighbours – ranking near the bottom of an index measuring levels of 'worker participation' of various kinds across Europe, ahead of only Bulgaria, Lithuania, Latvia and Estonia.[67]

By way of contrast, in the Nordic social democratic states of Sweden, Denmark, Norway, Iceland and Finland – known for their strong welfare systems –institutionalized unions still play a major role in economic and labour market planning.[68] These countries have high levels of union membership (the vast majority of workers) and sector-wide agreements. Elected union representatives negotiate directly with associations of employers to set pay and conditions for 70–80 per cent of all private sector workers (with the exception of Norway, which is closer to 50 per cent).[69] The collective agreements are binding and usually involve 'peace obligations', meaning that during the period of the agreement, disputes have to be negotiated and settled without strikes or other types of industrial action.[70]

One of the things that sets the Nordic model apart is the prominence of collective bargaining over statutory means of regulating working conditions, for example through national minimum wages. The high levels of organization of both workers through unions and employers through associations requires little state intervention. As a result the Nordic countries have relatively flexible labour laws when compared to the likes of France or Italy, which have instead tended to enshrine their workers' rights in law.[71]

In Germany, unions have an institutionalized role through industry agreements, as well as participating in 'works councils' which are associations of employees and management. This approach of 'co-determination' also includes the right for workers to sit on the boards of companies – the roots of which lie within grassroots union organization, but are today often synonymous with corporate management aims and boosting workplace productivity.[72]

Institutional unionism is often celebrated by Anglo-American unions operating in their comparatively austere and isolating labour markets. And for good reason – these models were hard won by unions and have produced remarkable levels of wage and gender equality for decades. But these models are in an almost universal period of decline. The political influence of European trade unions on policy making – even in the Nordic states – is falling.[73]

This is perhaps unsurprising given the international nature of neoliberalism and the corresponding models of financial capitalism. The EU became a vehicle for its advancement,[74] with guidance routinely including demands for wage moderation,[75] urging member states to ensure wage increases are part of an 'employment friendly policy mix' and that 'vigilance is needed over the impact of wage-settlements and labour-cost increases on price competitiveness'.[76]

Adhering to recommendations in the wake of the financial crash, several countries diluted their collective bargaining structures by either discontinuing national agreements, breaking up multi-employer bargaining or changing the rules around which workers are covered by sectoral agreements.[77] Compounding this, national policy changes over a longer period have meant that few countries now support union membership directly through public policy. Those that still do – the nations that adhere to the 'Ghent system', where unemployment benefits are accessed via union membership – tend to be smaller economies (Iceland, Sweden, Finland, Denmark, Belgium).[78]

We can't turn back the clock

One of the reasons that the ambition of re-establishing institutional unionism remains popular within sections of the labour movement is the promise of a return to the 'golden era' of post-war union strength. If unions have a seat at the table, then could the steady wage increases and labour share gains that existed during this period be recreated?

This thinking risks being clouded by nostalgia. The broader socio-political context of the post-war era in the UK and the US worked strongly in unions' favour. A major reason why capital owners were more willing than usual to work with unions during this period was the staggering rate of economic growth. Company bosses were more willing to agree to higher wages when they were also seeing their profits increase. Furthermore, in the context of the threat of international communism and a working class who had just made major sacrifices during the war, bosses were keen to do what they could to temper revolutionary impulses. Moreover, in the UK, whilst this era of relative economic equality and prosperity was enabled by progressive, Keynesian economic policy and strong unions, the scale of its success was only possible because of a much uglier economic reality: Britain's empire. Colonial rule resulted in a direct subsidy to British living standards by the nations it colonized long into the twentieth century,[79] a context that is often ignored by those celebrating the economic success of the post-war consensus.

With the additional imperative to reduce consumption in the face of climate change, global economic growth beginning to flatline, and the prospect of intensified rent-seeking, progressive movements will need to accept that a return to high levels of growth is neither possible nor desirable. This suggests that, rather than relying on 'win–win' solutions between capital and labour, unions may need to be more adversarial in their approach.

The truth is that today's economy bears less and less resemblance to the textbook scenario on which traditional, twentieth-century union bargaining strategies are based. Capital owners still rely on the daily labour of workforces to profit, and work is still the main site in which for most people the interests of capital and labour meet, but beneath this lies a raft of changes that undermine the position of workers.

Rebuilding an institutional role for unions in today's economy

Despite the renewed energy and interest in institutional unionism, the recent failure of democratic socialist agendas to gain electoral success in the UK or US means that unions in these countries won't be winning institutional power through a top-down policy programme any time soon. In both countries, due to historically low levels of membership and militancy, the other route to rebuilding institutional power – by negotiating sectoral agreements directly with employers, sector by sector – also feels far off. Significant victories are conceivable in legacy sectors like transport and utilities where union density is higher, and this should of course be pursued. However, on its own this strategy holds little hope for swathes of the most marginalized workers, in outsourced services, hotels, warehouses, supermarkets and call centres.

There are other limitations to this ambition. Collective bargaining over wages, which is the bread-and-butter practice of these institutional models, will not alone reverse the inequalities that have emerged under financialization.

Clearly, increasing the reach of collective wage-bargaining – and therefore wages – will help. After all, some of the mechanisms by which financialization has undermined the power of workers are partly an issue *because* of low wages. If unions were in a position to more effectively bargain for and win higher wages, then people wouldn't be in so much debt and would be better able to afford high rents. Furthermore, sectoral bargaining overcomes some of the corporate practices that undermine union solidarity – outsourced workers, for example, could be brought into agreements so that distant, unaccountable employers would no longer be able to duck union demands.

And yet, however far-reaching wage-bargaining agreements are, they do little to reduce the concentration of power underlying economies today, which is to be found in the realms of finance and capital ownership. When more and more of the economy is focused on financial markets, the portion of economic growth workers are able to access via bargaining for higher wages is reduced, and this is true whether we're talking about workplace or sector-wide bargaining. Furthermore, financialization has increased housing prices in some regions so much that wage increases would have to be substantial before homes were genuinely affordable. Even London's underground tube drivers, who are widely vilified in the right-wing media for their 'eye-watering' salaries won through 'unjustified' strike action,[80] can't afford to buy a house anywhere near where they work without an inheritance to set up them up. As one National Union of Rail, Maritime and Transport Workers (RMT) member and tube driver put it, 'If we, as unionized, organized public sector workers with wages far above average can't afford a house near where we work, what chance has anyone else got?'[81]

The hard reality is that collective *wage*-bargaining, for all its benefits, does little to stem the unequal growth of wealth and generational inequalities emerging from financialization. Some of the countries celebrated for the lowest global levels of *income* inequality and high union participation are in fact also home to some of the highest levels of *wealth* inequality. The Netherlands and Denmark are up at the top of the table on some measures of wealth inequality, with only the US ahead of them.[82] Sweden has higher wealth inequality than France, Germany and the UK.[83]

The Nordic states have also seen some of the biggest rises in income inequality in recent years, much of which is attributable to a widening gap between income from capital and income from wages.[84] Between 1980 and 2017 the top 1 per cent in Europe captured 17 per cent of growth, and the average income of the top 0.001 per cent of the richest Europeans rose by 200 per cent.[85]

The crux of it is this: wage-bargaining wasn't set up to deal with the type of capitalism we have today. Even strong wage-bargaining regimes struggle to maintain power against finance capitalism. In the 1950s Sweden adopted a union-backed 'solidaristic wage' policy to narrow wage differentials within and between workplaces – and it had strong success across the 1960s and 1970s, resulting in a steep decline in wage inequality.[86] But as union economist Rudolf Meidner recounted in his 1993 essay 'Why did the Swedish model fail?', the effect of the model tailed off in the later years of the century, and inequality in Sweden started to grow once more. Many things contributed to the model's decline, including the shift from large Fordist workplaces to smaller firms, and the increasing popularity of managerial control based on pay hierarchies.[87] But for Meidner, the ultimate failure of the wage solidarity model was down to an underlying design fault – it was not able to ensure that workers got their fair share of the firm's *overall* income. As the wages of workers were moderated and equalized, profitable firms paid out more and more of the company's wealth to its owners.[88] This case demonstrates the challenge for workers, even those with substantial institutional power, of trying to foster more equality in an economic system that is wired to enable vast inequalities of wealth to emerge. As we will discuss in chapter 4, Meidner and colleagues later sought to replace this model with one that tackled not just wage distribution, but wealth distribution too.

Democratizing the economy requires rank-and-file union strength

> It feels like a lot of ideas for changes to legislation to support unions are the icing on the cake, but the cake is the power of the union itself.
>
> UK union organizer[89]

To return to our original conundrum: what comes first, institutional power or organizing power? Ultimately, curbing the power of finance and improving legislation for workers requires an overhaul of the rules of the economy – many of which only a state can enact. But lessons from the past and the present day show us that this project must start, as most real change does, from below. A democratic socialist government will only get to power, and be effective in power, with a strong union movement behind it. If progressive governments are the political arm of the labour movement, then they are only as powerful as the workers they represent. In the context of an international wave of far-right electoral successes, led by oligarchs who game democracy and flirt with fascism, it is even more imperative that we rebuild the strength of unions from the bottom up.

This doesn't mean that work on a transformative policy programme should halt. Movements are sustained by ideas, ambitions and demands – which they themselves will also generate.

Once in power (at national, local or federal levels), policy makers who are serious about building a sustainable economic transformation should aim not only to build the institutional power of unions, but also to pursue legislation that supports the growth and strength of the grassroots.

Bolting sectoral bargaining onto a movement that is struggling to be fully representative of the workforce, with low membership and organizing capacity, may do little to really build union power. Structural, discursive and organizing power must also be addressed.

First and foremost this must include defending and strengthening the right to strike. Outsourced and gig economy workers striking against their de facto employers – be it a platform giant, a hospital or a government department – offer an important example of how even under a hostile policy regime, structural power can be leveraged. As we will see in the next chapter, it is US teachers who are popularizing striking again, and progressive politicians who are committed to democracy should be taking note and seeking to better protect and extend those rights in law.

Other ideas for legislative changes to support grassroots activity include compelling employers to afford their workers paid time away from their duties to participate in democratic workplace activities. Under this policy, these additional 'worker hours' would supplement the time shop stewards already have.[90] Combined with full access to workplaces for any union representative, this repurposing of working hours could catalyse new activity and union branches in corners of the economy that the movement is struggling to reach. In addition, forcing companies to operate more transparently, for example by publishing financial information, debt balance sheets and board notes, and holding open negotiations with unions, would begin to address the information imbalance that puts workers at such a disadvantage. These are powers that don't have to wait for national governments. Mayors, local politicians and unions themselves could be making these demands, guided by the aim of equalizing the means to organize between workers and capital owners, wherever the opportunity arises.

While these various legislative changes would make unions' jobs easier, there's work that can be done in their absence. In the rest of the book we'll explore where unions, instead of waiting for permission, are already stepping up to take a central role in democratizing the economy.

3

Bargaining with finance

> Reality check to teachers union: affordable housing has no place at the bargaining table
>
> *Chicago Sun-Times* headline[1]

On 15 November 2019, Chicago teachers agreed a new contract, ending an eleven-day strike and one of the most intense labour battles of recent US history. During daily rallies that drew thousands of supporters, teachers made an impassioned case that there was plenty of money to invest in schools, it was just concentrated in the wrong hands.

Their demands were diverse. Increasing wages was important, especially for school staff whose average annual salaries were low enough for their children to qualify for free school meals. But the teachers were fighting for much more than that. They were fighting for racial and economic justice for themselves, their students and their wider community.

After days picketing in the snow and rain, they won not only an increase in teachers' pay but also smaller class sizes, a social worker and nurse in every school, and a commitment to prioritize funding for schools that serve the most at-risk students. Racial and migrant justice was at the core of their demands, and after long negotiation, the City agreed to give sanctuary to undocumented migrants on school property.

Chicago is part of a wave of teachers' strikes that took off across the US in Republican as well as Democratic states, with astonishing success. In many ways their methods are age-old. Their success lay in months (sometimes years) of deep, skilled organizing through one-to-one conversations, and their primary weapon was the labour strike. But they also demonstrate some important strategies for how to bargain with finance in twenty-first-century capitalism.

Chicago teachers knew they had little leverage if they focused on their immediate bosses, Chicago Public Schools (CPS), whose budget was tight. For years before 2019 teachers had been doing their homework, exploring why a city that is home to some of the wealthiest people in America had such chronically underfunded schools. The answer lay in the stitch-up between elected officials and their corporate and financial funders.

The teachers exposed the way in which CPS had bought risky 'interest rate swap loans' from the Bank of America, Goldman Sachs, the Royal Bank of Canada and Loop Capital. These had looked like a good deal before the financial crash, but when interest rates were slashed post-2008, they became a liability, with CPS paying 3.66 per cent interest while the banks paid the Federal Reserve close to zero. The city lost almost $100 million, while the banks profited handsomely.[2] As Chicago activist and strike supporter Amisha Patel explained, 'Renegotiating these swaps could save CPS tens of millions of dollars every year – money that could keep schools open. But that would mean putting the interests of poor, black children ahead of the banks, a difficult move for a mayor whose top campaign contributors come from the financial services industry.'[3]

The teachers also exposed tax increment financing (TIF), a shadowy public financing tool that was supposed to be for 'blighted neighbourhoods' but was instead diverting tax money towards big developments, including the Chicago Mercantile Exchange at the heart of Chicago's Wall Street. When, in 2011, teacher Jackson Potter was arrested in a peaceful protest against the practice, he explained 'I told police I would have done it again . . . Big business is taking resources away from schools and working families, and we want it back.'[4]

By drawing widespread attention to the financial industry's exploitation of public schools, the Chicago teachers politicized the issue of public cuts, making clear they were not an economic necessity but a political choice. This meant that when, in 2019, just a decade after the biggest banker bailout in history, mayor Lori Lightfoot told schools they would have to 'live within their means' and the city wouldn't 'bail them out',[5] everyone could see this hypocrisy for what it was.

The teachers also took aim at Chicago's financialized housing system. In a particularly radical move, they demanded a host of affordable housing policies including teacher housing programmes, advocacy by CPS for the financing of social housing, and full funding for Section 8 (government assistance with housing costs).[6] These policies aimed to tackle decades of gentrification that has deepened inequity, particularly for students of colour. The policies weren't just campaigning points;

they were literally included in the teachers' 2019 contract negotiations.

In the end, the teachers compromised their housing demands to end the strike. However, the inclusion of housing in the contract negotiation suggests an important tactic for bargaining with finance. Unlike workers at Tops or General Motors (GM), which have been gutted by finance, Chicago teachers *do* leverage real power – without them, the state faces the embarrassment and disruption of closed schools. By bringing housing to the bargaining table, Chicago teachers started to use that leverage to wield power in another crucial site of economic extraction. As the union reported, the 'contract battle offers a new tool to protect our students and their families'.[7]

The Chicago teachers are not the only workers taking aim at finance. Across our economies, bank workers, grocery store staff, pension holders and renters are coming up against its oppression and finding ways to build power against it.

Unions in and for the community

Over the past few decades finance has spread into every pore of the economy, finding new and innovative ways to concentrate wealth and power through infiltrating our workplaces, homes, personal finances and public services, and moulding the system itself to its own advantage.

In order to tackle such an opponent, the labour movement, too, must be expansive, nimble and ambitious, using a variety of tactics in its aim of building economic democracy and power. This means organizing people as workers but also as members of communities, recognizing that they have relationships and struggles beyond their working lives. It means joining the dots between the financial protagonists who dominate our working and non-working lives, as well as our political systems. It means leveraging power across systems of oppression, wherever they occur. It means, where necessary, organizing unwaged people – who are, after all, about half the population – including some of the most economically marginalized, such as unpaid workers and those unable to work, who are key actors in the struggle for economic justice. It means firmly setting our sights not just on ameliorating the worst impacts of financial capitalism, but on building power for a broader economic transition.

These principles have threaded through the history of the labour movement. In Britain in the first half of the nineteenth century, for example, newly forming unions campaigning for better factory conditions joined the Chartist movement – a mass working-class movement aimed at democratizing the economy through universal manhood suffrage and other demands.[8] The movement was genuinely diverse, focused on building a social and cultural movement, and using strikes to build pressure for its demands. Although Chartism failed to achieve its immediate aims, it raised the consciousness of a whole generation. William Cuffay, an activist tailor and son of a slave, remarked that although 'as a trade unionist he had exerted himself', it was through Chartism that he became 'convinced that the cause of their distress was higher than the tyranny of their employer'.[9] The message was clear: set your sights not only on the ills of workplace exploitation, but on the system that enables it.

US unions in the 1930s aimed for similarly broad social, political and economic transformation. The broad-based strikes of 1933 and 1934 by communist-led unions created the pressure that led to the passage of the National Labor Relations Act, the Social Security Act and the Fair Labor Standards Act.[10] This was a period of deep organizing, in which rank-and-file workers acted as organizers in both their workplaces and their communities.[11]

While today many unions in the US and UK are narrow, service-oriented organizations, these elements of what is sometimes referred to as 'social movement unionism'[12] never died and are now on the rise. In the US this has manifested in the 'Bargaining for the Common Good' movement, a network of unions, community groups and racial justice organizations. They are aimed squarely at an overhaul of the system that keeps whole communities down. 'The campaign doesn't end once the union settles its contract', the website declares:

> Bargaining for the common good is about building long-term community-labor power, not about giving unions some good publicity during a contract fight. The boss doesn't automatically become a good actor once the contract is settled and the community's demands don't become any less important.[13]

In the UK, aspects of social movement unionism are being championed by small 'challenger' unions, such as the Independent Workers Union of Great Britain (IWGB) and United Voices of the World (UVW), which, for example, set up language classes and social spaces to build strong, often international, communities around their campaigns. Some larger unions also operate beyond workplaces, such as Unite, the UK's second largest union: in 2012 it launched 'Unite Community', a network to welcome members, including those who are unemployed, into the union for nominal rates. Unite Community branches aim to work on issues such as welfare injustice, high rents and disability discrimination, using a union organizing model.[14]

In the context of reduced structural workplace power, and the increased importance of non-workplace economic exploitation, the aims and tactics of social movement unionism become particularly important. Trying to tackle financial capitalism only through workplace organizing is like trying to fight an army by focusing on only one regiment, while the others ravage everywhere else. A union movement serious about democratizing the whole economy has to use leverage wherever it can be found.

Mobilizing the whole bargaining unit

A crucial way to maximize structural power (and a key part of social movement unionism) is mobilizing the whole bargaining unit. That can mean including subcontracted and outsourced workers in bargaining at a workplace level. This is one of the strengths of industrial unionism, which aims to unite different groups of workers within the same company or sector, compared to craft unionism, which organizes workers according to profession or skill. Even where workers are in separate unions, they can work together, as when outsourced cleaning and security staff at the University of London, who are part of small, independent union IWGB, joined with academic staff in the University and College Union (UCU) in a landmark strike in 2019, substantially increasing their structural power.[15]

Given the globalized nature of financial capitalism, mobilizing the whole bargaining unit also means building union campaigns across the value chains of transnational companies.[16] One international confederation of unions, IndustriALL, is trying to do this across the global automotive industry, which has a long and complex value chain in which one car company alone engages as many as 40,000 suppliers across the world.[17] IndustriALL plans to focus initially on car battery manufacturing because of the growing electric vehicles industry, serviced, until recently, by mining companies in the Democratic Republic of Congo using child labour to extract cobalt. This type of international organizing across different sectors and jurisdictions is a crucial but hugely difficult task. Networks of suppliers are deliberately opaque – hiding the fact that the further along the value chains, the less workers are unionized, and the worse the conditions.[18]

However, expanding the bargaining unit also means looking beyond workers altogether. It means drawing power from everyone who is affected by a workplace decision, including the people workers heal, protect and educate, or who buy the products of their labour. This is exactly the method used by Chicago teachers, who would never have been able to sustain such a prolonged period of industrial action without mass support from parents and community members.

As Saqib Bhatti, an expert on unions and Wall Street, puts it:

> If the corporations have found ways to make the labor part of their business less and less relevant, we need to figure out how we are also building power. One way to do this is by expanding the number of lives that bargaining touches, so that we can actually take corporations on in a meaningful way. That means going deeper with community members who are impacted by those corporations and their behaviour.[19]

This can be a particularly valuable method for those in insecure work. Last year, UK McDonald's workers went on strike for a wage of £15 an hour, security over hours and the recognition of their union, the Bakers, Food and Allied Workers Union (BFAWU). However, they struggled to attract enough strikers to shut down the six restaurants affected. This is because fast-food workers and other hospitality workers are often employed casually and regularly have to move between jobs , making building long-term workplace campaigns and effective actions hard. The union movement struggles to reach them, and even when it does, a missed day's pay or the fear of getting on the wrong side of management presents too much of a risk. To overcome this lack of organized power, hospitality workers across a number of chains have begun building local support networks, so that the risks (and potential wins) of their actions are shared. As South London-based bartender and union organizer Amardeep Singh Dhillon explains: 'We are involving our friends, families, neighbours, local mosques, churches and other union branches. We might be insecure in work, but already have deep roots and networks we can rally for support in our communities.'[20]

Through this independent offshoot of the union, volunteer organizers like Singh Dhillon are raising local awareness, building strike funds and inviting pro bono help from their neighbours. Singh Dhillon describes this as 'territorial organizing'. 'As a community,' he explains, 'we have a claim over our shared spaces. We have given over our high streets to major companies like McDonalds and Wetherspoons in exchange for jobs that leave us struggling to pay rent or live any kind of comfortable life. Together we can resist it.'[21]

Using workplace power where it still exists

Some workers have more structural power than others. Although financialization has reduced the power of many workers today, others still command substantial leverage. In our globalized goods market, logistics workers are crucial.[22] Vast 'logistics clusters' of transportation hubs, warehouses, distribution centres, seaports and airports use huge workforces and sophisticated technologies to handle and direct the importing and exporting of goods. In the US this brings tens of thousands of workers into densely packed areas, often just outside of major cities and towns, who could bring the economy grinding to a halt if they went on strike.[23]

Some service workers also have substantial structural power. This most obviously includes skilled public service workers such as teachers and healthcare workers, and it's no coincidence that, in the US, it's teachers who have led the charge against finance. Although lower-paid service workers are often considered structurally less powerful because they are generally easier to replace, they too can wield significant leverage. This applies particularly, for example, to care workers in the private sector, on whom, with an ageing population and more parents at work, our economy increasingly relies. If used properly, their embeddedness within a community, and their relationships with the parents, patients, students and neighbours they service, could offer modern-day service workers an *advantage* over more traditional factory-floor style organizing, making it easier to mobilize the whole bargaining unit in a fight. In many areas of the service economy, the site of production *is* the community.[24] Furthermore, many of these jobs are impossible to offshore and less immediately vulnerable to automation or artificial intelligence than many other professions.

One important strategy for the labour movement is to leverage maximum power where workers still have it, not only to improve their wages and conditions, but also to make *other* demands from financial elites and regulators, just as the Chicago teachers did by making housing a contract issue.

The idea of expanding the scope of bargaining is a key principle of Bargaining for the Common Good, and is being picked up across the US.[25] Increasingly, workers are bringing issues related to racial discrimination or environmental justice to the bargaining table. But they're also taking aim at finance. In Minnesota, teachers demanded as part of their contract negotiations that the district stop all business with banks that foreclose on families with school-aged children during the school year. Although the Board of Education didn't agree on these terms outright, the teachers did get them listed as a 'statement of intent' in their employment contracts.[26]

While most examples are in the public sector, one private sector example is the organization of US bank workers. The Committee for Better Banks is a coalition of bank workers' unions and community organizations working to reform banking.[27] Their work has included fighting sales targets which force workers towards predatory sales practices – effectively pressuring people to take on loans they can't afford, disproportionately affecting people of colour and those on low incomes.[28] In 2016, Wells Fargo workers exposed the bank's cheating scandals, and in 2019 they forced chief executive officer (CEO) Tom Sloan to resign, by blowing the whistle on the bank's reinstitution of toxic sales goals during a congressional hearing. In 2018, Los Angeles bank workers successfully pressured the city to adopt a 'responsible banking ordinance' that requires any bank bidding for the city's $17 million public contracts to disclose any sales goals or predatory practices. As Ruth Landaverde, a former Wells Fargo and Bank of America worker, explained:

> We took power away from big banks and their army of lobbyists and gave it back to the people of Los Angeles . . . This rule is the result of advocacy from thousands of Los Angeles bank workers and residents and serves as a blueprint for cities across the country that want to wipe out big bank behaviours that prey on working families.[29]

While financialization provides more ways for company owners to make money without directly employing many workers, the finance firms themselves rely at some level on co-operation with workers, who could themselves be unionized. The payday loan industry relies on workers to administer their shop fronts. Even hedge funds and real estate companies rely on some more poorly paid staff, who, like the workers in the

Committee for Better Banks, could be unionized to resist the predatory practices of their employers. In this way, we can effectively start regulating banking from below.

Targeting the real boss

Multiple layers of subcontracting complicate the relationship between employee and employer. If you are a subcontracted worker, your direct boss might only have tiny profit margins, despite the fact that someone, somewhere is profiting handsomely from your work. Subcontracting is effective not only in creaming off profits for managers and shareholders but also in isolating workers from the people with real control over their wages and conditions. As one UK organizer put it, 'under outsourcing, workforces are seen as a service, as costs to be driven down'.[30]

One of the first examples of workers getting to grips with this challenge was the US Justice for Janitors campaign in the 1990s. Janitorial services were a heavily subcontracted industry with very poor working conditions. If workers demanded more, the building owners could easily move to another subcontractor. Instead of organizing by subcontracted company, workers started organizing by geographical area, through a series of parallel campaigns with workers at different contractors, meaning building owners could no longer play them against each other. Once workers across contractors were organized towards a common goal, they could target the real boss (for example, the Philadelphia Electric Company, which owned buildings the subcontracted janitors cleaned) through strikes or other action and leverage real structural power. Through these methods, the Janitors were able to win substantial increases in wages and better conditions.[31]

Twenty years later, outsourced workers are facing similar challenges. In 2018, the UK union IWGB went to court to challenge the fact that outsourced workers at the University of London were not being allowed to bargain with their de facto employer (the university itself) but only with their direct employer (Cordant Security). The union lost that case, but nevertheless had their sights firmly set on their real boss, laying the groundwork for the joint UCU and IWGB strike in 2019. As former outsourced worker and union president Henry Chango Lopez argued, outsourcing 'is no more and no less than a way to deny workers their rights, and it is about time we cleaned it up'.[32]

Leverage shareholder power

One strategy for workers to gain power is to go straight to the top, by pressuring – or actually becoming – shareholders in the companies that employ them. In 2015, nearly a quarter of independent shareholders at the transport company National Express annual general meeting backed a resolution for an independent inquiry into anti-union activities in Durham School Services – one of the company's US school bus subsidiaries.[33] This case was part of a campaign by the Teamsters union to get shareholders on side and force National Express to meet the demands of its US bus drivers. Durham School Services is one of the largest US school bus systems, with tens of thousands of workers who for years have raised concerns of labour law violations, such as wage theft and anti-union tactics during organizing drives.[34] The campaign forced the company to sign a memorandum of understanding with Teamsters, though disputes over the treatment of their workers continue.

A union trying to organize in Albertson's, a major US grocery chain, took an even more direct approach. The United Food and Commercial Workers International Union (UFCW) bought forty-three shares in the company so they could raise resolutions in the company's shareholder meetings. They submitted motions to declassify the board of directors (so they would have to stand for re-election), and built up leverage by buying shares in other companies in which the company directors held stock. Their proposals gained some support from other shareholders, but were ultimately dismissed on the grounds that they were not acting 'in the interests of the stockholders', but rather to 'pressure the Company to unionize its Arizona employees'.[35] The campaign nevertheless had some success, and some local stores now recognize their union.

Although it's easy to think of shareholders as the super-wealthy, most workers indirectly hold shares in pensions. These funds are crucial in oiling the financial system, with the US and UK holding the largest pools of retirement assets in the OECD.[36]

Pension funds are often invested in ways that seriously undermine workers' rights, but there's substantial variation between countries. Looking across Europe, most pension funds have explicit policies to support labour rights (in the Netherlands, Denmark and Sweden, many even have specific clauses to exclude companies such as

Wal-Mart and Ryanair because of labour rights abuses). But of those pension funds that don't, *three quarters* are held in the UK.[37] By funding companies that deny worker rights, workers are often, through their pension funds, unknowingly colluding with their own subjugation.

In the US, unions have a much stronger role in managing private pensions and so also a much stronger history of shareholder activism.[38] These are not always restricted to issues of worker rights. Recently, for example, the California Faculty Association pressured their pension fund, the California Public Employees' Retirement System (CalPERS), to sell its stock in two private prison companies that operate detention facilities at the southern US border for the federal government. Margarita Berta-Ávila, the group's associate vice president, said the union 'was not going to stand by and watch our pension dollars support these terrible corporations'.[39]

Unions can also be proactive about saying what pension funds should be used *for*, and not just what they are against. The UK's major university union, UCU (which recently led a fourteen-day strike across over seventy universities), has set ambitions beyond simply defending the members' academic pension. They want to turn the pension into 'an ethically invested, socially responsible scheme that combats, rather than accelerates, climate change' and are also campaigning to extend the scheme to all lower-paid and casualized staff.[40]

Shareholder activism has been criticized by some as offering an alluring but misguided 'shortcut' to worker rights, diverting efforts from deep, workplace organizing.[41] Where such activism is being exercised exclusively, and in the place of on-the-ground organizing, this is certainly a risk, and admittedly major gains from attempts to sway shareholder power have been few and far between. But instead of seeing these strategies as an 'either/or', they must be 'both, and'.

Finance is multifaceted and requires multifaceted responses. Far from being a *replacement* for worker organizing, shareholder activism is another weapon in the arsenal for workers, part of a network of pressures that can force companies to act more democratically.

If workers themselves start to get more familiar with and able to lead on these shareholder strategies, the results could be immense. Finding out that the major shareholder of an outsourcing company where workers are organizing also owns shares in a privatized care home that a sister union has recognition in, for example, is valuable information. Similarly, discovering that a union pension fund is propping up an exploitative employer could be a campaigning tool to build awareness and activism among that union's rank-and-file members. There is a massive opportunity for political education. Understanding and uncovering how corporations are working behind the scenes, their links into the financial system and who is really making the decisions is a critical step in building worker power. In many cases workers are taking the initiative and finding these things out for themselves, but the education departments of unions could play a crucial role in scaling up this work.

Collective bargaining outside work

Under financial capitalism, unaffordable housing costs and personal debt are as debilitating for many people as low wages and poor-quality work. However, any site of extraction is also a site of leverage, and in recent years there has been a small revival in collective organizing around rent and debt, often with crucial union support. Any union seriously organizing around the concerns of their workers, and exploring their structural causes, will come across these issues sooner or later. This doesn't mean that unions must necessarily *lead* organizing in these areas, but supporting or joining forces with these struggles is a crucial way in which the labour movement can pursue its aim of democratizing the economy.

Collective bargaining over debt

For many, the age of finance is experienced as an age of debt. One of the successes of modern capitalism is to instil the belief that debt is sacrosanct and not to repay it is effectively stealing. However, in the post-2008 era, this fiction has become harder to uphold. As governments paid trillions in banker bailouts, it was suddenly clear that we don't *all* have to pay our debts. Some people began to recognize personal debt burdens for what they are: structural problems, not personal failures.

Founded in 2014, the Debt Collective has its roots in Occupy Wall Street. One of its early projects was the Rolling Jubilee – what the Collective termed 'a bailout by the people, for the people', in which they bought and cancelled medical and student debt – over $31 million worth to date.[42] In 2015 they ramped up their action, organizing a debt strike against for-profit Corinthian Colleges. Corinthian exemplifies the link between financialization and racial capitalism – their recruiting tactics disproportionately targeted people of colour, working-class and Latinx students. The company were already under investigation for fraud and predatory lending, and the debt strike, combined with mass legal action, led to Obama's Department of Education discharging almost $1.5 billion in debt from former Corinthian students.[43]

Collective organizing around debt has real potential to disrupt the current economic system. As John Paul Getty apparently said: 'if you owe the bank $100,000, the bank owns you. If you owe the bank $100 million, you own the bank.' As debt activist and anthropologist Hannah Appel explains, 'The starting point for debtor organizing is to ask what would happen if we saw the staggering $13.5 trillion in total household debt as a source of collective leverage, rather than aggregate individual liabilities.'[44] Symbolically, the threat of non-payment, not as debt 'forgiveness' but as an economic injustice righted, threatens the very principles of debt sanctity upon which financialization rests.

Given the lack of legal protection for debtors (compared to, for example, striking workers), choosing to stop paying your debts is a high-risk strategy. And yet for many it's not a choice: people are *forced* to default on their debts. The real choice is whether to politicize this as collective action, as students at Corinthian Colleges did, or to suffer alone and in silence.

Given the financialization of non-financial firms, it's easy to imagine how labour unions could work with debtors. Imagine, for example, the recent strike at GM. The strike lasted forty days, involved 48,000 workers and cost GM up to $2 billion. But with profits at $25 billion, GM held tight and the strike was only partially successful.[45] Meanwhile, its financial arm – GM Financial – is one of the US's biggest lenders of car loans, with an increasing number of debtors behind on repayments. 'Imagine if we had a GM debtors' union set up when GM plant workers went on strike, and debtors went on a solidarity strike', suggests Appel; 'it's a perfect example of the kind of complementary organising that needs to take place in the era of financialization in order to strengthen factory floor organising.'[46]

While choosing not to pay debts during a period of economic stability can seem like a tall order, a crisis can provide the political opportunity that sparks the tinder. In 1994, steep inflation of the Mexican peso brought 30 per cent of people indebted to banks into default. The El Barzón movement responded by setting up legal consultation services for debtors and undertaking a variety of creative campaigns. The government were eventually forced to come to the aid of the debtors.[47]

Economic crises can also open up possibilities for resisting mortgage debt. When the bottom fell out of the US sub-prime mortgage market in 2007, the subsequent wave of repossessions was met with a strong response from a network of activist, community groups and labour unions. Tactics were creative, ranging from blockading evictions against heavily armed SWAT teams, making so much noise in auction rooms that foreclosed houses couldn't be sold, and staging protests at banks profiting from the housing system.[48]

Spain saw similar community efforts to stave off evictions. Platform of Mortgage Victims (Plataforma de Afectados por la Hipoteca, or PAH) consisted of self-organized groups who blocked the evictions of families facing home repossession, where punitive Spanish laws on not repaying your mortgage meant not only losing your home, but also being in debt to the bank for their legal fees and the mortgage, plus the difference in property value due to devaluation. Worker solidarity played an important part in both cases. In Spain, community activists were even supported by firefighters in some cities who refused to assist evictions.[49]

One recent study from the New York Federal Reserve suggested that something approaching an informal and unofficial debt strike did occur in 2007 in the US. The study found that when home equity turned negative, people tended to prioritize repaying credit cards and other loans like car finance over mortgage repayments.[50] In other words, as Americans watched their home values plunge, some made the decision to stop paying their mortgages.

This was a calculated decision based on the premise that when debt bubbles become too bloated, the problem of that debt can shift, albeit in some cases momentarily, from the debtor to the lender. The study found that as the number of defaults rose during the unfolding recession, it was taking banks a long time to make their way through the repossession process, meaning that people were not at immediate risk of eviction. In most cases, the tactic didn't achieve much beyond allowing people to spend an extra few months in their home.[51] Nevertheless, this decision by some to simply stop paying their debts illustrates how a crisis can become an opportunity to reframe what debt means and to mobilize debtors against their creditors.

Collective bargaining over rent

There is a rich history of rent strikes on both sides of the Atlantic. In the UK, a rent strike in London's East End helped win the Dockers' Strike of 1891, and the Glasgow rent strike of 1915 forced the government to introduce rent controls for the first time in the private sector – both strikes led by women.[52] In the US a history of rent strikes culminated in a wave of strikes in the 1960s and 1970s, led by people of colour who were in part protesting the deeply racialized private rented sector.[53]

After a quiet few decades since the 1980s, rent strikes are starting to make a comeback. A small spate of rent strikes have occurred across California, including Westlake,[54] San Francisco and half a dozen in the rapidly gentrifying areas of Los Angeles and Cleveland, Ohio.[55] These have had some success. A nine-month rent strike in Boyle Heights, Los Angeles, in the face of 60–80 per cent rent increases, won a three-and-a-half-year rental agreement for a 5 per cent increase a year and a commitment to renegotiate when the agreement runs out. 'They won protections that are equal to rent control', Tracy Jeanne Rosenthal, co-founder of the LA Tenants Union, says. 'By themselves they did the work that policymakers refused to do.'[56] Over the border in Toronto, rent strikers won another key victory against rent increases from landlord MetCap in 2017.[57]

There has been less activity in the UK, with the only major rent strikes in recent years those by students living in student accommodation. Rent strikes kicked off in University College London in 2016, and were followed by strikes at the Courtauld Institute of Art, and Roehampton, Goldsmiths and Bristol Universities, with many winning substantial reductions in rent increases.[58]

The UK has also seen a small resurgence of renters' unions. As the private rented sector has grown, some tenants are getting organized, and demanding radical change to the barely regulated, unaffordable and insecure rental market. The London Renters Union was set up in 2016, and ACORN, a 'community union' with a strong focus on housing, and branches in a growing number of cities, in 2014. Fed up with charities providing advice or politely lobbying their local council, these unions are aiming to create a new model of power.

The UK's atomized model of landlordism makes organizing rent strikes particularly challenging; the average number of properties owned by a landlord is two or three, far fewer than in the US with its larger-scale, professionalized landlords.[59] This makes it hard to build a critical mass of renters against a particular landlord, or to get serious improvements for many tenants with a single large-scale action, as rent strikers have been aiming to do in US apartment blocks. Interestingly, recent policy initiatives in the UK encouraging a 'build-to-rent' approach may lead to more concentrated landlordism, with large-scale developers likely to increase their percentage of the market. By increasing the proportion of renters who share a common landlord, this could, ironically, make it easier to build resistance to the financialized private rented sector.[60] At the moment there's more emphasis on creating campaigning and solidarity actions (for example, members repeatedly blocked the phone lines of an estate agent in a mass 'phone picket' until the agent repaid an unfairly withheld deposit to one of their members)[61] than actual rent strikes. Nevertheless, this organization could be crucial in building the solidarity and political identity required to start building towards bigger action.

Organizing across sites of extraction

Organizing around debt and rent isn't easy. The internalization of debt as a shameful failure makes it hard to build a political identity – a crucial foundation for collective organizing and the ability of a movement to build discursive power. Without legal protections, debt and rent strikers risk affecting their credit score – a fate that can upend your future life chances, and a major mechanism by which financial elites maintain economic discipline.

But no organizing worth doing is easy, and many of the things that are supposed to make workplace organizing easier, such as the political identity of 'worker' and legal protections (which are themselves being chipped away,) only exist because they were built through hard organizing.

Despite the obstacles, *when it's seriously attempted*, it's not clear that organizing around rent and debt are less effective than workplace collective bargaining. Without any of the political support, infrastructure, institutional power or funding that the labour movement has at times laid claim to, some debtors and renters have won real material improvements through their action. The Corinthian College strike played a critical role in forcing an entire college to declare bankruptcy, cancelled $1.5 billion in debt, and can take substantial credit for the fact that a number of democratic politicians – including Bernie Sanders – openly support student debt cancellation. That's all on the back of one strike and four years of organizing.

While they might not be best placed to lead the charge to organize around debt and rent, labour unions can both strengthen these struggles and use them as one weapon in their arsenal. Work could involve consciousness raising among their members to promote synergies between campaigns and even solidarity actions.

It could also involve organizing their own members around other issues; for example, a health workers' union could take action over student debt incurred by its members, or a union organizing low-paid service workers could take action over payday loans. Just as the financial system extracts wealth on a number of fronts, the labour movement, too, must be ready to resist on just as many fronts.

These kinds of synergies were supported historically in the UK with a series of 'trades councils'. These are regional bodies which bring together different unions and community campaigns focused in one area, and were established in the nineteenth century. They aim to 'promote effective solidarity in disputes, joint campaigns on issues such as health, education, welfare and transport, and, in general, provide the vital link between the workplace and the wider working-class community'.[62] They have in the past been the home for coordinated grassroots actions including union support for rent strikes, organizing community support for mass pickets, and coordinating local arms of general strikes. Today, save for a few active branches, Britain's trades councils are largely defunct, but either they – or equivalent models – could be crucial in linking together campaigns across issues.

Building militant, democratic, intersectional unions

It's noticeable how many of the most inspirational union actions documented here have been carried out by workers independent of, or explicitly against, their union hierarchies. The militancy of the Chicago

Teachers Union, for example, was initiated through study groups and organizing outside official union activity, with workers eventually running an internal slate in 2010 against what had become a complacent, concession-prone union hierarchy.[63] Amardeep Singh Dhillon and his colleagues in the insecure hospitality sector have ended up organizing outside union structures so that they could be more nimble.

Not only are many unions failing to organize for serious militant action, their restrictive hierarchies can actively hinder action. As Daniel Randall, railway worker and National Union of Rail, Maritime and Transport Workers (RMT) activist pointed out, most UK union branches don't even have the power to organize their own industrial action: 'they have to get permission from the wider union, and often this means distant officials sat in a London office. Union bureaucracies have in effect invented their own anti-strike laws, on top of the ones the state is imposing.'[64]

In 2018, the campaign group Justice for Cleaners, made up of outsourced university cleaners and students, called a series of demonstrations to put pressure on the London university Goldsmiths to in-house their staff. The local branch of another, much larger union actively distanced themselves from the protests, writing an email threatening that any strike would be illegal, only later supporting the campaign.[65] These disputes between unions are not uncommon. Larger, established unions are often reluctant to recognize the wins of the sometimes risky but often highly effective actions of their smaller counterparts. While this book has focused on structural reasons why unions are struggling to win power, we must also accept that some of the responsibility for that decline must rest with issues arising from within the union movement itself.

Although pockets of important action will continue, these are unlikely to grow to the scale needed without a concerted renewal and democratization of unions themselves. It's essential that, as unions refresh their ambitions towards democracy in the economy, they do so internally too.

Part of this process must be to address deep-seated issues of representation. Unions are failing to properly represent marginalized workers both in their membership (members remain older than the average worker and migrants remain under-represented in the US and the UK[66]) and in their leadership, with women poorly represented, and people of colour even more so.[67]

As Ian Manborde, equality and diversity organizer for the union Equity, puts it: 'The profound social and workforce changes around the dynamics of class, race and gender pose significant challenges, and opportunities.' The fact that 'trade union leadership and staff remain relatively static despite this shift is one key measure of why trade union power is diminished'.[68] This inevitably leads to biases in whose interests are represented.

This lack of representation across union hierarchies has implications for action too. As one UK union organizer succinctly explained, 'the officers in my union are pale, male and stale. If they were standing in front of me asking me to take action, I'm not sure I'd have much confidence.'[69]

One of the manifestations of sexism and racism in the labour movement has been the disproportionate value put on male, skilled, often white-dominated occupations (the 'aristocracy of labour'), at the expense of those in more precarious, female and migrant-dominated sectors. Even those unions, or branches of unions, which use aspects of social movement unionism and focus explicitly on marginalized workers aren't necessarily immune to undemocratic practices, for example maintaining disproportionately male-dominated leadership.

An urgent priority of union renewal must be building a movement that deserves the trust of the most marginalized workers, particularly those of colour. A first step is recognizing the depth of harm that has been done by unions' racist past and the enduring reality of racism in the union movement today.

Union researcher Stephen Ashe has written about the numerous, 'often overlapping' reasons why non-white union members in the UK rarely turn to their union for solidarity, despite being more likely to be members of unions.[70] This includes their experiences of direct racism from officials, collusion between unions and managers to conceal racist practices in workplaces, and an unwillingness to name and address racism from within the union's membership.[71] But there is also a bigger failure by the movement to recognize the working class as being multi-ethnic and multi-racial and to evolve its structures, strategies and leadership accordingly.

If unions are going to seriously become the organizing arm of the whole working class today, they need to be relentless in organizing against attempts by the owning class to pit racial groups against each other. This is only going to become more important with the rise of the far right in response to climate migration. This means taking a strong pro-migration line and resisting arguments such as those pedalled during Britain's

Brexit campaign that fracture working-class solidarity in favour of 'white working-class' identity, even when these attitudes are expressed by union members. As well as recognizing and calling out racism within the union movement, we could simultaneously do more to recognize how much the union movement owes to migrants and people of colour, with many of the most innovative organizing tactics imported from the Global South, or from the civil rights movement.[72]

The lack of representation of young people is also a major weakness. Not only does this mean the movement is failing to adequately represent some of the most marginalized workers, but it also spells serious problems for membership rates – and dues – as older workers retire. As Becki Winson puts it, 'Every trade unionist under the sun sees this, and is in a panic about it', and although recent campaigns, particularly among hospitality workers, are showing that young workers can be recruited and organized, 'no one has yet worked out how to do this on a large scale'.[73]

Whilst the big unions are ploughing funds into researching how to access young people, with mixed results so far, young people themselves are organizing. As we have seen from the recent climate strikes, young people are far from disengaged – an estimated 1.4 million young people from across the globe were prepared to take organized, collective action against ecological injustice.[74] The transatlantic democratic socialist agendas have inspired mass participation and leadership in political projects by young people, such as in the Democratic Socialists of America in the US, and Momentum in the UK. If even a fraction of these movements saw unions as a vehicle through which they can realize economic justice, it could significantly grow the labour movement over just one generation.[75]

The broader challenge of democratizing unions is beyond the scope of this book, which is focused on external structural power, rather than internal organizing power. But the bringing together of workplace and community-based actions *should* be a chance for unions to address some of these issues, offering the opportunity to link workplace justice with issues of gender and racial justice, as has been such a central theme of the Bargaining for the Common Good movement.

Those who have always had to struggle harder for democratic representation and economic justice should be those whom the union movement seeks to learn from and follow. Women have taken a strong leading role in historical rent strikes – the home being a traditionally female realm. Majority women and migrant workforces in the care economy – whether childcare or elderly care – are subject to low-pay, high-insecurity conditions. In the gig economy it is again women and migrant workers who dominate the workforces of emerging care and cleaning apps.[76] Rather than these groups being written off as 'unorganizable' in a changed world of work, they should be the priority of any movement with the ambition to rebalance economic power – as the 8,500-strong women's strike of cleaners, caterers and clerical workers in Glasgow recently demonstrated with their historic equal pay win.[77] It's no coincidence that many of the existing 'green shoots' of creative union activity have been actions led by migrants, women or people of colour.[78] It's a manifestation of what happens when grassroots-led action cuts through and forces the issues of those most disempowered, within work and the economy more broadly, to the top of the agenda.

4

Owning the future

In November 2008, ABC Learning, the world's largest listed childcare provider, went into voluntary administration. The Australian company, which at its peak had nurseries across Australia, the US, Indonesia, the Philippines and Hong Kong, collapsed after recording a mammoth annual loss. ABC provided care to tens of thousands of children, and 16,000 jobs, and the Australian government decided that it was too big to fail, investing AUD 56 million to keep its doors open until a new buyer could be found.[1]

What went wrong? Founded in 1988 by entrepreneur Eddy Groves and his wife Le Neve, ABC Learning was part of a tide of corporate investment in childcare. In 2001, ABC Learning was floated on the Australian Stock Exchange and grew aggressively, borrowing heavily to buy and build new nurseries, crowding out local competition and buying up chains abroad. The firm achieved near-monopoly status in some areas of Australia.[2]

ABC's growth was enabled by a rare combination of financial opportunity over the preceding decades. Demographic shifts saw childcare demand surge as parents left family networks to pursue jobs in quickly expanding cities, and more women moved into work.[3] A wave of deregulation also allowed private providers to profit from subsidised childcare places. This was ushered in by a corporate lobby which, in 1991, objected to 'discrimination against the private sector' caused in part by unionized nursery workers with 'unnecessarily high' qualifications driving up the cost of providing childcare.[4] The subsequent changes to childcare funding and licensing resulted in a surge of childcare provision in private centres, which, between 1991 and 1996, shot up by 233 per cent.[5] The changes sparked a huge flow of money from the state into private childcare chains, with one study estimating that between 2005 and 2006 ABC received over 200 million Australian dollars in public subsidies via childcare benefit payments.[6]

Meanwhile, the withdrawal of public funds for nursery construction helped push up the asset value of licensed nurseries to such an extent that, as one government report put it, 'real estate acquisition and income from rents from childcare centres was the "raison d'etre" that led corporate players to invest in childcare'.[7]

By 2006, Eddy Groves was the richest man in Australia under forty years of age, and the financial pages of the press were full of admiring commentary on the corporation.[8]

However, ABC relied on an army of overworked, underpaid, insecure and almost entirely female workers. Standards and pay were notoriously poor. Financial records from before the collapse revealed that, even in its 'boom days', ABC only spent 56.7 per cent of its revenue on staff, compared to an average of 80 per cent spent by not-for-profit providers.[9] Childcare workers at the firm reported having felt entirely disempowered in their jobs, owing to a 'corporate culture of secrecy' and having little control over their hours.[10]

In February 2008, ABC's poor management and over-optimistic expansion caught up with it. Heavily loaded with debt, it faced a 40 per cent slump in profits from which it couldn't recover. After it went into voluntary receivership, officials discovered highly questionable accounting practices that had grossly overinflated the company's value. Years of financial investigation followed, with Eddy Groves finally going bankrupt, although the only real scalp from the investigations was former chief financial officer James Black, who got a suspended sentence.[11]

ABC's rise and demise made it a classic case of the financialized firm: its business model relied on heavy indebtedness, asset-price inflation, share-price supremacy and worker exploitation. Although Australia-based, ABC is emblematic of a general tendency towards the financialization of childcare – and care in general – in Anglo-American countries, with finance-backed private providers in the UK and US increasingly dominating the market, and private equity and overseas ownership featuring heavily.[12]

However, ABC was also a missed opportunity. Despite being side-lined by a financialized ownership model, workers in this sector do have substantial structural power, as they are crucial to the functioning of the rest of society. That's why the government had to step in and save it. What would it have taken to use the crisis to democratize the childcare sector? At the point at which the Australian government had to buy out the chain to keep the nursery doors open, what would it have taken for parents and workers to be ready to pool resources and buy out their local branch at a discounted rate? Such a transition could have democratized a large portion of the sector and radically shifted the power away from finance and towards parents and workers. As we will explore in this chapter, unions could play a critical role in seizing on moments of weakness when finance falters – and using them to democratize ownership. This is particularly valuable in sectors such as care which are heavily financialized, provide a critical role in the economy, and are dominated by poorly paid, undervalued and mostly female workers.[13]

A renewed role

Unions have a role not only in resisting the worst excesses of financialization and rent-seeking in the existing economy, but also in building a new one. Unions could provide the institutional clout, legal support and organizing capacity required to support worker and other forms of democratic ownership (such as public ownership), particularly in sectors that we rely on day in, day out. These endeavours can not only improve the lives of workers and communities today, but also build the foundation of a more democratic economy of the future.

Democratizing ownership

Under financialization, the ownership of the means of production, assets, wealth or intellectual property becomes concentrated in fewer and fewer hands. One of the promises of neoliberalism was a vision of a share-owning democracy, which British prime minister Margaret Thatcher described as a society in which 'owning shares was as common as owning a car'. In fact, business ownership in the US and the UK has concentrated and moved offshore.[14]

Democratizing ownership is a key way of transcending financialization. A radical change to the structure and ownership of privately held firms and assets would not only cut off rent extraction at source; it would also give workers and customers more levers to shape the purpose of new institutions and industries that can be tasked with socially and environmentally useful activity.[15] Democratic ownership is particularly important, as it defines who benefits not only now, but also in the future. Targeting wages alone will never rebalance power and wealth in the economy to the extent that's needed. These imbalances are set to deepen as automation and artificial intelligence are predicted to replace mid-level jobs most, pushing more people into low-paid, low-skilled work.[16] With financialization limiting the success of wage-bargaining, worker ownership could help insulate workers' incomes in a near future of increased automation and an intensification of rent-seeking. In most businesses, increases in productivity from technology might decrease the need for workers. However, a business owned by its workers could harness increased productivity to increase leisure time or ensure incomes over a longer period.

Unions are well-known advocates for increased state ownership over key industries. They played a central role in developing the ideology behind the British welfare state post-1945, and the rapid growth of shop steward organization in the 1960s and 1970s, particularly in manufacturing, encouraged a renaissance of the debates on workers' control which had flourished half a century before.[17] Today there is a renewed appetite for bringing various private industries and assets back into public hands, with strong interest in the progressive left in the UK, and also in the US despite its much weaker history of state ownership. But this appetite is for a form of collective ownership that looks different from that of the past.[18]

State ownership of the kind prevalent in post-war Britain – while ostensibly more democratic than the market – was part of a top-down nationalization programme which kept most of the private sector bosses in place.[19] This type of nationalization does little to increase the power of workers or their communities over an industry. It works at a scale that is vulnerable to corporate capture and can be quickly reversed with changes in political leadership, as evidenced by Thatcher's astonishingly fast sell-offs in the 1980s.

In the UK between 1974 and 1976, unions used the opportunity of a progressive Labour government to push for more democratic models of public ownership and the nationalization of shipbuilding, aircraft, land and financial institutions.[20] Although shipbuilding was nationalized, the plans to incorporate worker control were not enacted by the time there was a change in government.[21]

Building on these attempts and learning the lessons of the past, more recent proposals have advocated more devolved ownership, with stronger forms of democratic governance and accountability.[22] These include municipal and locally led models where decisions and benefits directly involve the people that work in the businesses or live near them, as well as models that seek to combine elements of worker, state and common ownership. One prominent proposal is 'inclusive ownership funds'[23] – a model to 'consistently and over time' transfer the ownership and control of businesses to workers and stakeholder groups, which was adopted as Labour Party policy in 2019, with Bernie Sanders adopting a similar demand as part of his leadership bid.

These policies take inspiration from an idea developed by Swedish trade unionists nearly fifty years ago: the 'Meidner Plan'. In 1973 a working group of union officials and economists drew up an evolution of the Swedish wage solidarity model, which (as discussed in chapter 2) was designed to equalize the differentials between wages of workers in high- and low-profit sectors. The new plan had to do three things: complement this wage policy in such a way that wage moderation would not in turn enrich the owners of high-profit firms; counteract the concentration of private capital; and strengthen employees' influence in the workplace through co-ownership.[24]

The working group devised a plan to gradually pass company shares into a worker-controlled fund. Over time, the workers' share of the company would increase until they became majority owners. The idea was taken to the annual national union congress in 1976, where it was met with huge applause from the conference floor. As Meidner recalls, it was as though 'an issue had been created capable of mobilizing and activating the union movement'.[25]

The plans were, however, never fully realized. Political leadership changed and a watered-down version was delivered years later by the 1983 socialist government, whereby funds were set up but there was no attached ability to socialize the ownership of the companies. By 1989 they had accumulated substantial capital – SEK 22.7 billion (around $3.8 billion)[26] – and were dissolved soon after under a centre-right government. After some debate about whether or not the union movement, as the initiators of the plans, laid claim to the fund, the government directed its use towards research and subsidies for pensions.[27]

Despite the labour and co-operative movements having similar roots and principles of democratic organisation, they have important distinctions in their approaches and a somewhat uneasy history. This could be through collective bargaining in private sector workplaces to win a gradually increasing stake of ownership, through facilitating worker and state buy-outs of collapsing firms, or through supporting the setting up of worker-owned, unionized co-operatives from scratch.

Despite the labour and co-operative movements having similar roots in industrialization and sharing a strong emphasis on member control through democratic practices, they have a somewhat uneasy shared history.[28] The relationship between British co-operative and union movements of the nineteenth century was close. Many co-operative movement activists had supported Labour's emergence as a fully independent party in 1918, as the political arm of the union movement. Once in power, however, Labour focused on nationalization as the ownership model of choice, and the two movements drifted apart. [29]

Today, some union activists are wary of worker co-operatives, viewing them as attempts to smooth over the inevitable and constructive conflict between labour and capital. Co-operatives are private businesses, and although they are based on democratic principles, they do not automatically recognize unions as a key part of their operations. Any increase in un-unionized worker co-operatives would reduce union membership and broader attempts to build industry-wide solidarity. In the US, scepticism wasn't helped by a movement in the 1980s and 1990s by some unions, such as the United Steelworkers (USW), towards employee ownership, exchanging contract concessions for ownership stakes in order to keep the business afloat. These often failed to secure significant improvements, and came to be seen as another way to placate and rip off workers.[30]

Co-operative ownership can be lumped in with a broader set of 'financial participation' initiatives, including management-controlled schemes for profit-sharing or employee share options – neither of which implies a meaningful democratization of ownership or governance.[31] Furthermore, not all co-operatives are what they seem. For example, 'The Co-operative Group', a large UK consumer co-op, operates without any genuine worker democracy and is in fact listed on the stock exchange and owned by shareholders.[32] These models hurt the reputation of the co-operative sector and instil scepticism within the union movement. However, this should not detract from the potential of genuine, worker-led initiatives in democratizing ownership.

Becoming worker-owners

Unions could play a central role in pursuing democratic ownership through collective bargaining. Just as they negotiate a 5 per cent increase in wages, for example, workers could negotiate a percentage of shares in the company. In the absence of institutional power (a state willing to legislate for the democratization of ownership), this strategy relies on workers' structural power. Just as in the Meidner Plan, progress might feel small, but incremental changes could have huge effects over time.

By using an employee fund model, such as in the Meidner Plan, any voting rights of workers gained through becoming shareholders could, in theory, be transferable to a union – a way of ensuring that collective interests in company governance take primacy over individualized ones. This approach would give worker funds an institutional home – and could also resolve one of the big problems with the Meidner model, which was the very large disparity between dividends from high-profit and low-profit sectors. Unions could be a vehicle to pool incomes from dividend-rich sectors to fund deeper organizing in communities, and also among sectors with high levels of workers and lower profits, such as care.

In addition to transitioning towards collective ownership gradually, unions can also have a role in establishing new, entirely worker-run union co-ops. Union co-ops differ from regular worker co-ops in that workers are unionized, with a separation between governance and management responsibilities. Workers bargain with an appointed management team to set wages and conditions just as they would in any other unionized workplace. This also provides the mechanisms for grievances and arbitration of workplace disputes. As worker-owners, unionized employees gain equity in the business in addition to wages. This model has been developed and promoted by the USW union in the US, in partnership with Mondragon, the vast Basque union co-op.[33] 'Too often we have seen Wall Street hollow out companies by draining their cash and assets and hollow out communities by shedding jobs and shuttering plants', explained USW president Leo Gerard in 2009. 'We need a new business model that invests in workers and invests in communities.'[34]

Mondragon is by far the most famous, and largest, union co-op – a vast cluster of 256 companies covering manufacturing, engineering, retail and financial services. But there is a wealth of other smaller union co-ops that are less well known.

Cooperative Home Care Associates (CHCA) is a social care agency based in the South Bronx and employing almost 2,000 home care workers, most of whom are African-American or Latinx.[35] CHCA is a union co-op with the explicit aim of economically empowering low-income New Yorkers through demonstrating what work can look and feel like when you are collectively your own boss. Home care workers can participate in decisions by attending quarterly regional meetings, serving on the board of directors or worker council or becoming a union delegate, and are paid for their time to do so. Workers collectively decide on the split between income and wages each quarter.

CHCA isn't perfect. Only about half the workers have made the investment to become owners (a $50 initial investment, and then a small regular payment out of their pay packets), and democratic participation is relatively low.[36] However, the company demonstrates viability in exceptionally hard circumstances – working in an endemically poorly paid industry and recruiting from a neighbourhood experiencing generational unemployment. In this context, the fact that they have managed to be profitable for over thirty years, and to maintain staff on substantially better pay and conditions than the sector average, is testament to the potential of the model.[37]

Currently, the co-operative movement is small – just 1 per cent of business turnover in the UK,[38] and a fraction of the co-ops are unionized. In the US in 2019, worker co-ops employed just 6,500 people – almost one third of whom worked at CHCA.[39] And yet they are an enduring part of those economies, providing good-quality and meaningful work, whilst demonstrating a different way of doing things. In the US the number of co-ops is also growing substantially, led predominantly by women and people of colour (particularly Latinx workers).[40]

Unions are particularly well placed to play a role in growing the sector. One of the most common methods by which co-ops emerge is through 'business succession' – workers taking over a business when an owner is ready to move on. In the UK, there are around 120,000 family-run small and medium enterprises expected to undergo a transfer of ownership in the next three years, and these could be ripe for worker takeovers. .[41]

Business succession towards worker co-ops can happen in different ways. At times it can be a smooth process in which business owners choose to transfer ownership to their employees – such as when Linda and Gregory Coles sold their New York day-care centre, A Child's Place, to their staff in 2018.[42] It can also be more turbulent, such as when workers at Chicago company Republic Windows and Doors faced redundancy.

When it looked as though the company was going to close without paying workers proper redundancy, the unionized workforce staged a sit-in until they were paid what they were owed. Some of the staff then used this money, combined with additional money from a non-profit fund, to buy the machinery and establish New Era Windows Cooperative, a union co-op.[43]

As democratic structures already operating within the workplace with expertise in human relations, in management and in finances, unions could also assist the set-up of new co-operatives, or support workers to co-operatize existing businesses. This support could involve forming an organizing committee, researching a business plan, finding funding sources, preparing the legal structure and documents of incorporation and offering training.

Unions (including Unite, the UK's second largest union) played such a role for aircraft manufacturers in Yorkshire in 2011 in a little-known, and ultimately unsuccessful, case. Following threats that the site would close, with 899 job losses, unionized workers devised a plan to pool their redundancy money and take it over as a worker-owned co-op. The plan was based on reviving the production of Jetstream planes, which had been manufactured for military use, for civilian use. Prospects were promising; the workers secured interest from an overseas airline company, negotiated access to the original production plans, were in advanced discussions about commercially renting the site or having it gifted to them as part of a handover deal, and 120 of them were lined up to pool redundancy money for a share buy-out.[44] As one organizer recalls, 'it seemed like the stars had aligned . . . We had the people, the facilities and the willingness to do this and it certainly seemed like it could work.'[45]

In the end, the main investor never followed through, and the workforce ebbed away as the redundancy programme reached its conclusion. As one of the architects of the scheme, Roy Cartwright, explained, 'We couldn't ask people to sink their redundancy payments into the project without having a firm order and ultimately we were left to wonder what might have been and watch hangars close and skilled fitters walk away from the industry.'[46] Roy had been a union convener and had worked on the site for over forty years. A year after the plan failed he reflected 'there's a real lot of sadness . . . without [the factory] there's nothing'.[47]

While the aircraft manufacturers' plans failed, they did so not because of an inherent flaw in the model, but because it needed stronger institutional support. Institutional support could be provided not only from unions but also through progressive local and regional governments. Even where national governments aren't supportive of these schemes, progressive politicians operating locally or regionally with devolved powers could work with unions to grow alternative ownership models. In Italy since the 1980s, worker-controlled enterprises have emerged from worker buy-outs, saving or creating substantial numbers of jobs through a transformation into co-operatives.[48] The difference between these Italian successes and the aircraft manufacturers is that in Italy, under the Marcora Law, workers have first refusal on buying the firms facing closure, and can access capital investment and technical assistance from regional and national states.[49] Emilia Romagna in Northern Italy is a hub for worker-owned enterprises, including a network of 'social co-operatives' (co-ops delivering elder, disability and other forms of social care).[50] Both unions and co-op representatives are involved in workplace, regional and national bargaining.[51]

Some of the most interesting examples of unions supporting the initiation of new worker co-ops come from the Global South, where co-operatives for free-lancers and mutual guarantee societies provide some of the social infrastructure required by growing self-employed workforces, including workspaces, childcare or healthcare provision.[52] The Self Employed Women's Association (SEWA) in India integrates the provision of work security, food security and social security in its definition of 'full employment', which it works to provide for its members.[53] Similarly, the Working Women's Forum in Southern India, a mutual association which works across several states alongside a union and a co-operative development service, has established a healthcare service, childcare, family planning and educational services.[54]

Unions as investors in the areas side-lined by capital

One of the impacts of financialization is the way in which it has held back productive investment in the 'foundational' economy – the distribution of everyday goods and services which we all need to live a normal life.[55] These are the un-sexy parts of the economy that tend to be locally rooted – calling out plumbers, couriers, finding last-minute school uniforms, or providing home care.[56] While exploiting opportunities to profit in some areas of the foundational economy (particularly care services and supermarkets), capital investment has otherwise tended to concentrate in regions with more high-end consumption, or in technology and finance sectors – spilling across London and the UK's South East, or in the US clustered around bi-coastal 'superstar' cities. Combined with deindustrialization, the neglect of the foundational economy has hollowed out whole regions of these wealthy countries – leaving towns with abandoned high streets, little public transport and closed public services.

Under neoliberalism, a misguided 'market knows best' ideology meant that there has been little explicit industrial planning that could have corrected these sectoral and regional inequalities. However, in the aftermath of the financial crisis, and with automation and climate change looming, there has been a renewed interest in interventionist industrial strategy in both the US and the UK, at least rhetorically.[57] Nevertheless, many proposals so far are deeply disconnected from the communities they claim to serve.

Modern industrial strategy generally relies on technocratic 'predict and supply' models, where the state intervenes so that the requirements of the evolving economy and technologies can be fulfilled. However, nothing guarantees that new industries conveniently match the skills, interests and geographical distribution of displaced workers. Take truck drivers, for example. Driverless vehicles could become mainstream relatively soon, and could be both safer and more fuel efficient. However, in the UK there are nearly 300,000 people employed as truck drivers that could find themselves redundant.[58] Overall, it is hoped that this kind of technological unemployment can be compensated for with new jobs in high-tech, high-skill industries – such as IT, biotechnology or robotics. As former UK prime minister Theresa May outlined in a speech in May 2018, it is 'science' which is at the 'heart of a modern Industrial Strategy'.[59] But while this approach might balance labour market statistics on a spreadsheet, it will do nothing for former truck drivers. These workers tend to be older, with low educational opportunity, and in the absence of high-quality career support or affordable adult education, new careers in a digitalizing economy are likely out of reach.

An alternative approach is to ask how a new economy can be shaped so that it fulfils social needs and enhances the wellbeing of the workers involved and society in general. This requires a shift from asking what workers can do for the economy, to asking what the economy can do for us.[60] The answer will be different in different communities and regions. To really design an economy that is more equitable and responsive to local needs, economic planning needs to be radically devolved.

Unions could play a crucial role in this process. Building on traditions of community organizing while innovating new methods for democratic participation in economic decision-making, unions are uniquely well placed to engage meaningfully with workers and their communities.[61] This could be usefully combined with a role for unions as investors in and supporters of new models of ownership. These initiatives could be focused first and foremost on the foundational economy.

Take post offices, for example. In the UK, post offices offer more than just a postal service. They offer passport applications, bill payments and banking services and are often the only amenities in rural areas, providing a crucial hub for the community. They are particularly vital for small businesses, and for people less able to travel.

The privatization of the Royal Mail – the UK's major postal service, which had been in public hands for 500 years – sparked widespread opposition, including from the union that represents postal workers, the Communication Workers Union (CWU). Despite the Royal Mail being a profitable business, having undergone modernization and automation reforms, a Conservative–Liberal Democrat coalition government argued it was a 'financial basket case' (commercially unviable), and sold it off at a substantially undervalued share price in 2013.[62] A series of subsequent job losses and branch closures (with more to come) left many communities and workers stranded.

Today the CWU is paving the way for worker ownership of post office sites across the UK, as a way to both protect the livelihoods of postal workers and embed the union in the communities they seek to support and represent. The union is approaching city mayors and other local decision-makers to build support for a new model. Many post office branches currently operate as small independent franchises, with the Post Office Ltd providing equipment. This could provide a low-risk model for a co-operative structure that requires limited up-front capital investment, forming an important exemplar for unions taking a lead role in democratizing ownership of a critical public service.[63]

As well as creating new jobs and businesses, unions can play a role in building democratically owned housing. Proliferating union-owned or union-supported co-operative housing could be one way to remove housing from the financialized marketplace and create buildings that are homes, not just financial investments. Unions, in fact, have an interesting history in doing so.

Today, more than 100,000 New Yorkers live in apartments built by the labour movement between 1926 and 1974, including through a coalition of unions and community organizations set up in the 1950s and known as the United Housing Foundation.[64] The co-operatively owned housing units were open to any worker earning below a certain income, unionized or not. Around 40,000 of the homes are still affordable, co-operative units today. Union organizer Erik Forman writes that the move into housing provision, which had roots in a Yiddish communist group called United Workers and a socialist club for Finnish immigrant workers, 'was as much a political project as an economic one', encompassing 'a 20,000-volume library, regular cultural and political programming, and involvement in the broader community through a network of co-op businesses, political support for local tenants and workers, and attempts at racial integration'.[65] The developments were funded by equity investments from local residents, topped up with loans from the union-affiliated Amalgamated Bank, which still operates today.[66] A life insurance company provided an additional $1.2 million mortgage, and cultural and religious associations secured extra finance to plug gaps.[67] The project inspired other Jewish left organizations to launch similar initiatives, which, as Forman writes, 'turned the Bronx into a hub for experiments in working-class co-operative housing'.

More recently, a union co-op development organization in Cincinnati is one of several groups behind a rental share scheme that allows low-income renters to acquire equity in their property and take part in decision-making over the wider estate. The project has the explicit aim of tackling racial inequality whereby working-class black communities are locked out of secure, affordable rental housing and home ownership, contributing to the country's dramatic racial wealth gap.[68]

By supporting, financing and initiating democratic ownership of workplaces and housing, unions can occupy the sectors and regions that capital has either side-lined or exploited, effectively implementing an industrial strategy from below.

Unions leading the move away from damaging work

Unions need not only to tackle financialization but also do so in a way that can support climate change mitigation and be robust to carbon reduction. While workers and unions are often criticized for acting as blockages to a green transition, many workers recognize the need to move away from damaging work and are willing to take a lead in doing so if the support is there.

Unions have a long history in supporting this transition. In 1975–6 a collective of unionized workers produced an Alternative Corporate Plan for their workplace, the Lucas Aerospace Corporation. In response to cuts in the British defence budget, Lucas Aerospace had been offshoring and 'rationalizing' its activities, resulting in the potential for significant redundancies. Together, through a joint union initiative, workers put forward an alternative plan to transform the use of the capital infrastructure towards the production of a range of socially useful goods, which would also protect jobs.

Their strategy, which came to be known as the 'Lucas Plan', is today revered as an exceptional attempt to use worker ingenuity and organization to shape economic activity.

What makes the Lucas Plan exceptional is workers' recognition that the cuts to defence budgets were desirable, despite the risk to jobs. Rather than simply campaigning against the cuts, they argued that the 'traditional method of fighting for the right to work' was losing its power, citing that between 1960 and 1975 the aerospace workforce dropped from 283,000 to 195,000 – a result of a trend in which industries were 'tending to become capital intensive rather than labour intensive with structural unemployment in consequence'.[69]

The Plan was developed by a Combine of unionized workers formed across affected workplaces, including staff and manual workers from the company's seventeen sites across the UK.[70] The Combine had initially been established by shop stewards to enable workers to have a coherent voice in negotiations. Their remit began to extend way beyond this, becoming a hub for education and sharing of ideas about the future of the industry. By overcoming traditional union structures, based on geographical and skill divisions in the craft union tradition, the Combine was able to wield considerable power in the context of a large, complex firm.[71]

The Plan – described in a 1976 *Financial Times* article as 'one of the most radical alternative plans ever drawn up by workers for their company'[72] – eventually hit a series of walls, with opposition from both management and parts of the leadership of the unions involved. Though never realized, the Lucas project had ripple effects in the UK and internationally.

In Germany, for instance, the Lucas Plan inspired a metalworkers' union to establish 'Alternative Product Working Groups' in a number of firms. Workers proposed ideas for sustainable heat and power systems, transport, and tyre-recycling equipment. To support their proposals, 'Innovation and Technology Centres' were set up in some cities in collaborations between unions, universities and local authorities.[73]

In the US, in 1977 the Defense Economic Adjustment (DEA) Act, sponsored by former Democratic presidential nominee George McGovern, proposed a new council of unions, non-defence businesses and government cabinet members to divert production away from defence.[74] Under the act, management, workers and members of the community would draw up conversion plans and funding would be provided. Workers converting from arms production would have been provided with a salary and benefits for up to two years, financed by a levy on defence contracts. Neither the DEA Act, nor similar proposals in other states that it inspired, passed at a federal level.[75]

At the time of writing, as the COVID-19 crisis unfolds, there are a number of examples of workers proposing transitions towards socially useful activity. COVID-19 seems to be hitting some carbon-heavy industries – particularly the aviation industry – particularly hard. In early 2020, workers in General Electric (GE)'s aviation division faced redundancies of 10 per cent of its domestic aviation workforce (some 2,600 workers).[76] Faced with these redundancies, alongside the need for a collective response to the pandemic, workers demanded that the massive factory capacity was repurposed to build urgently needed ventilators, while introducing strict measures to keep workers safe as they did so. As workers across a number of plants staged silent marches, carefully distanced six feet apart, the president of the International Union of Electronic, Salaried, Machine and Furniture Workers of the Communication Workers of America (IUE-CWA), Carl Kennebrew, explained that: 'Our members are ready to help America during this COVID-19 crisis by making life-saving ventilators in our IUE-CWA represented facilities. These workers have the skills, and we have the space in our plants to do this work. Instead of laying workers off, GE should be stepping up to the plate with us to build the ventilators this country needs.'[77] Workers are calling on Trump to require GE to repurpose its factories.

There are also examples of workers using industrial action in support of renewable technology industries. In 2017 two of the UK's major unions, GMB and Unite, launched a joint campaign to avoid the mothballing of two steel fabrication yards in Fife, Eastern Scotland. On receipt of notice that the yard was likely to go into administration following a cash-flow crisis, the remaining workforce staged a 'work-in'. Their demand was that the steel yards remain open for the production of parts for a huge new offshore wind farm being erected just ten miles away.[78] Despite this effort, in 2019 it was announced the major contracts would go overseas, with the parts being shipped hundreds of thousands of miles back to Scotland.[79]

In a similar case, in 2019 shipbuilders at Harland and Wolff, the iconic Belfast ship yard that built the *Titanic*, occupied their workplace for nine weeks when faced with closure, demanding the site be nationalized and focused on the production of renewable energy. This campaign had partial success. The yard was recently bought by a London company and jobs were reinstated,[80] although, without repurposing towards renewable production or changing its ownership structure, it is likely to fall foul of similar market forces in years to come.

Transitioning towards green jobs is not only important to ensuring that the labour movement actively contributes towards climate change mitigation. It's also important to ensure that, as our economy inevitably *does* transition away from carbon-heavy industries, as many workers as possible are protected from the fallout. This includes ensuring affected workers have a genuine democratic structure that allows them to collectively shape the terms of the transition. These examples show that a worker-led transition could form a key plank of a progressive green industrial strategy. However, the shortcomings in Belfast and Fife suggest that for them to work, these initiatives need stronger institutional support. While unions might not be able to bridge this gap alone in every case, they could be a crucial broker for local state and municipal support as more of these cases unfold.

Unions leading the fight for free time

As well as getting ahead of the curve when it comes to climate transition, workers also need to do so in regard to technological unemployment.

Marx's argument that there is an inbuilt tendency in capitalism to replace labour with machinery has stood the test of time, with deep economic shifts from the industrial revolution to the present, led by the introduction of new technology. However, substantial technological advancements in recent years haven't translated into overall job losses. Instead they have transformed the types of work we do, with new technologies replacing semi-skilled roles, which pushes more workers down into low-paid, 'low-skilled' work.[81]

However, just because technology has not seriously reduced the amount of work in recent decades, that doesn't mean it won't do so in the future. In the past, increases in productivity (and corresponding reductions in labour intensity) from new technologies have been compensated by increases in consumption. Given environmental constraints, this strategy may no longer be possible.

Furthermore, some economists argue that developments in artificial intelligence mark a distinctive break with previous technological changes, and its widespread adoption could have a deeply disruptive impact on the labour market. Unlike previous waves of technology, which have tended to replace manual jobs, artificial intelligence threatens jobs previously reliant on the human brain. Jobs traditionally carried out by women are particularly at risk.[82] These include online chatbots replacing service roles such as telecoms or desk-based customer services, or clerks and web developers replaced by virtual counterparts.

These combined effects of automation and resource constraints could spell a particularly challenging environment for job creation, and make it increasingly easy to imagine a future in which the demand for human work shrinks.

These changes aren't led by technology – they're led by people using technology. The problem is that those people are already powerful, and technological advancement often concentrates this power still further. The crucial challenge for unions is to shift from being on the back foot – defending jobs that are being automated – to being on the front – finding ways to shape the economic use of technology in ways that benefit workers.

The strongest response by unions so far is to argue for a reduction in hours. This includes a successful campaign by the CWU, which represents 134,000 Royal Mail postal workers, towards securing a gradual reduction in working time to thirty-five hours a week (down from thirty-nine) by 2021 without a loss in pay. As a direct response to the impact of automation, CWU argues that workers, as well as the company's shareholders, should benefit from the mechanization of the parcel packaging process. A similar argument is being used by Fórsa, Ireland's major public sector union, whose members recently voted in favour of a campaign to reduce working hours, following a decade-long pay freeze and increase to working hours under government austerity measures, despite technological efficiencies over the same period.[83] Cases like these are emerging internationally, including among Icelandic public sector workers, German metalworkers and Canadian car manufacturers, where unions have secured reduced hours and increased holiday, sick leave or caring leave.[84] Although wins so far have been sporadic (taking place at the level of an individual firm), UK unions are now considering sector-wide campaigns in manufacturing and the bus industry.[85]

The 'fight for free time'[86] has a long tradition in union campaigning. It was unions that won the weekend and the eight-hour working day through mass movements, with gains rolled out via coordinated action and the international strategy of the International Labour Organization (ILO). Crucially, these campaigns represent a response to automation that retains workers' structural power, with workers still able to carry out industrial action and shape the work that remains. Furthermore, the campaigns represent a new potential for unions in pivoting away from a position of defending work, to one that defends the freedom of workers *from* work with an increase in leisure time. Campaigns for a shorter working week are proving popular with young and women workers in particular, with arguments being made for a better sharing of good-quality employment between generations and genders. As Nadine Houghton, a national officer of the GMB union, puts it:

> As a union official you get caught in the trap of negotiating on pay, and we forget that control over our working hours and a reduction in working hours is something that could actually transform our lives. It's a demand on which the trade union movement was based and it's one we urgently need to revisit, not just because of the immediate improvements it promises, particularly for working parents, but because it has the potential to reinvigorate the movement.[87]

Campaigns for a shorter working week could not only improve the lives of workers now, but could also be catalytic in building a new democratic culture – both inside and outside of work. With more time, workers would have more capacity to participate in unions, learn new skills and become active in their communities. Where this kind of democratic, participative culture has existed in the past, it has been undermined through the economistic, individualist neoliberal project. The demise of community infrastructure in post-industrial areas is just one example. Rebuilding this kind of culture will be essential to successfully building green industrial transitions and new economic models at the scale required, and in a way that puts people and not new technologies at its heart. Reduced working time – combined with policies such as 'worker hours', described in chapter 2 – could help enable such a transition.

The re-emergence of working-time reduction campaigns among unions over recent years could be interpreted as a pivot by unions away from protecting jobs for their own sake, towards enriching lives beyond work. And it's one that proponents of 'anti-work' or 'post-work' agendas are emboldened by, as it forces us to question the social value of modern work – and for some, work in general.[88] Anthropologist David Graeber argues that many jobs are, by the admission of their workers, currently pointless.[89] These jobs are either in entire industries which seem to produce no real value or in new layers of bureaucracy and administration (for example, people in universities responsible for reporting activities in order to demonstrate competitiveness against other universities). These 'bullshit jobs', according to Graeber, represent not only a waste of time, but also a miserable working life for millions of people. Few people are happy doing pointless work, no matter how much they're paid.

Protecting existing jobs is part of the DNA of unions. Often, their role has been to make visible and venerate work, and to expose the power relations that underpin it, so that it is properly recognized and remunerated. The idea, then, that many of our current jobs not only will but in fact *should* die out challenges these values.

In a potential world with less work, unions are a

critical agent in ensuring workers aren't left destitute. However, if unions are going to remain relevant to a new generation of workers in the context of bullshit jobs, automation and a green transition, then they may need to embrace, rather than fear, a future with less waged work – using it as an opportunity to transform the work that remains. In doing so, unions could become as active in ending pointless or damaging jobs as they have been historically in protecting valuable ones. This requires unions to reach and empower workers across all sectors of the economy, enabling more people to choose and shape the work they do. Bullshit jobs will die out if no one can be forced to do them.

Unions as architects of a democratic future

Ultimately, state support is needed to force through the scale of change that's required to shift our economy from one which is finance dominated, to one in which democratic ownership dominates and workers have substantial control over their work and time. However, by taking advantage of crises (such as those at ABC) to support one-off shifts to democratic ownership, alongside bargaining for incremental increases in worker ownership in a larger number of firms, substantial progress can be made without state support. By increasing the number of workers, and voters, who have experience of both democratic ownership and union organizing, these initiatives could play a role in ushering in state legislation to support both. However well intentioned, top-down policy attempts to nationalize sectors or impose green industrial plans without worker consent and control built in are destined to fail. If the union movement is to undertake real renewal, it must take itself seriously as the architect for a democratic future.

Conclusion: a way forward

At the time of writing, the COVID-19 virus is sending countries into lockdown. As pandemic status has been announced by the World Health Organization, it's becoming clear that certain workers are indispensable to our recovery. Around the world, whole populations are relying on nurses, cleaners, supermarket workers, childcarers and couriers to limit fatalities. Stock markets are crashing and governments are scrambling to balance financial and economic interests with the need to stem the spread of the virus.

We don't yet know how this global health crisis will be resolved. What we do know is that the workers who are already faring the worst under financialization – those experiencing subcontracting, unliveable wages, high rents and debts, and distant bosses – are the workers keeping economies afloat. Those who can afford it self-isolate, whilst workers in our health and care systems, in low-paid self-employment, delivering food, driving buses, cleaning trains, keeping schools and nurseries open to care for the children of other essential workers while they go to work, are taking on the lion's share of risk. As a result, the virus is further entrenching health inequalities on the basis of structural disadvantage, with people of colour disproportionately losing their lives in both the US and the UK.[1] At the same time, this pandemic is revealing, as crises often do, the weaknesses of our current system: privatized hospital beds out of reach of public use and insecure workers, with no sick pay, unable to afford to stop working.

As markets flounder, insurance companies close their books and supermarket shelves are emptied, the collective voice and power of workers have never felt so important.

This crisis might appear to be testing economies to breaking point, but the writing was already on the wall. After decades of neoliberal hegemony, the old order is now beginning to crumble. The financial crash over a decade ago revealed the cracks in the ideology, and economies continue to fall under further strain from bloated debt markets, the climate crisis, and most recently a global pandemic.

Meanwhile, for a generation of workers disempowered under financial capitalism, the electoral route to change has proven ineffectual. Recent democratic socialist projects mobilized thousands on both sides of the Atlantic but have not yet come to fruition in the way many hoped they would. The legacy of these projects, however, is still full of latent possibility.

One such possibility is a momentous, renewed interest in unions as a vehicle for social and economic transformation. For this to be realized, the notion of unions as vehicles for narrow wage-bargaining must be abandoned. In an era when power is based on wealth, and when workplaces and the economy have been captured by perverse financial interests, the challenge of union renewal is much bigger than turning back the clock to the post-war era of union power. It is about building out into communities and combatting the insecurity and isolation of much modern work with solidarity from those who rely on it, including patients, neighbours, students and parents. It is about setting our sights high, on transforming our economy from one based on finance to one based on democracy.

The process of renewal

Whilst a global pandemic, climate change, automation, economic crises and intensified rent-seeking all threaten to further undermine worker power and deepen inequality, they also present opportunities to rewire the economy. Realizing this opportunity requires resistance to the oppressions of the current economic system, both in the workplace and beyond it. Through acts of economic disobedience, workers, renters and debtors can effectively regulate finance from below. Realizing this opportunity also requires a clear vision for a new, genuinely democratic economy. Crucially, this vision is not something that can be developed 'in theory' or implemented from above. It has to be built and adapted through a process of collective education and action based on a shared understanding of power. Union structures, institutional knowledge and resources are important tools in this endeavour, and ones that aren't being fully used.

Unions are in fact *the* critical agent in this project. Despite decline, unions still represent a sizeable mandate with democratic infrastructures that spread across workplaces, communities and regions. No other self-organized institution has such reach and potential to organize and mobilize – and there are already signs of a renewed movement emerging. Demands to reduce the working week could be a crucial catalyst in this process. If won, more free time for workers would enable people to better realize their potential as agents of social and economic change, and build their self-worth beyond paid employment. With more time for socializing, education and participating in their communities, workers become a stronger force for democratic change in both their workplaces and the whole economy.

This book's small contribution to union renewal is to explore the way in which finance has changed not just the way we work, but how and where we function as democratic agents in today's unequal economy. Financialization, we have argued, is a logical extension of the age-old system of capitalism, finding further ways to extract wealth and deepening its unequal power relationships. Only by forcing transparency, collective voice and worker control over more areas of the economy, and resisting rent-seeking wherever it occurs, can financialization be transcended.

Unions, as a means of creating solidarity with others in work who are experiencing the same oppressions, will survive any mutations of capitalism. Some of the statistics on union power might be dire, but there is no existential threat. Although the movement has been slow to adapt to some elements of this economic era, as long as there is work, there will be unions.

Union renewal is imperative, not just because unions are struggling to increase membership, but also because, to be an effective democratic force in the economy, they themselves need to be committed to enhancing their internal democracy. Democracy is a job that is never done. It means evolving structures and strategies to bring the most marginalized workers to the fore, and ensuring those in positions of power reflect and represent the membership at large. It also means enabling new unions to flourish in industries where established unions have so far struggled to make inroads. There are clear gains to having a smaller number of larger unions that are able to build a critical mass to wield maximum leverage and build institutional power. However, in order to foster a period of innovation, this may need to be combined with smaller, more autonomous branches and DIY unions which can try new things, make mistakes, and learn lessons from which both they and larger unions can benefit.

A creative renewal of unions is a challenging task, but it is a challenge we must meet if we are to overcome the dehumanizing impacts of financialization and democratize our society in the interests of all.

Notes

Introduction

1 'Wal-Mart the nations worst workplace bully', *People's World*, 23 January 2003, https://www.peoplesworld.org/article/wal-mart-the-nation-s-worst-workplace-bully.
2 Mark Anthony Martinez, *The Myth of the Free Market: The Role of the State in a Capitalist Economy* (Sterling VA: Kumarian Press, 2009), 38.
3 Martinez, *Myth*, 38–9.
4 James Call, 'Walmart sued for collecting life insurance on employees', *WFSU News*, 7 May 2010, https://news.wfsu.org/post/walmart-sued-collecting-life-insurance-employees; Martinez, *Myth*, 38.
5 Rana Foroohar, 'The allure of financial tricks is fading', *Financial Times*, 3 March 2020, https://www.ft.com/content/a9f13afc-3c3d-11e9-b856-5404d3811663.
6 Martin Arnold and Emma Dunkley, 'Warning signs emerge in the UK car loan market', *Financial Times*, 9 July 2017, https://www.ft.com/content/8b6607de-6304-11e7-91a7-502f7ee26895.
7 Susan Lund Jonathan Woetzel, Eckart Windhagen et al., 'Rising corporate debt: peril or promise?', Discussion

Paper, McKinsey Global Institute, June 2018; Martinez, *Myth*, 38.

8 Foroohar, 'Allure'.

9 Marisa Fernandez, 'A record number of U.S. workers went on strike in 2018', *Axios*, February 2019, https://www.axios.com/bls-labor-strikes-education-teachers-079c2e8c-0633-4b09-bc09-ee8cc3ba27a2.html.

10 Department for Business, Energy and Industrial Strategy (BEIS), 'Trade union membership statistics 2018', *Trade Union Membership: Statistical Bulletin*, 30 May 2019, https://assets.publishing.service.gov.uk/government/uploads/system/uploads/attachment_data/file/805268/trade-union-membership-2018-statistical-bulletin.pdf.

11 Bureau of Labor Statistics, U.S. Department of Labor, 'News release: union members, 2019', 22 January 2020, https://www.bls.gov/news.release/pdf/union2.pdf.

Chapter 1 How financialization undermines the power of workers

1 David Robinson, 'Tops plans to close 10 stores across the state it says are underperforming', *The Buffalo News*, last modified 31 August 2018, https://buffalonews.com/2018/08/30/tops-plans-to-close-10-stores-that-it-says-are-underperforming.

2 Eileen Appelbaum and Rosemary Batt, 'Private equity pillage: grocery stores and workers at risk', *CEPR*, accessed 16 November 2019, https://cepr.shorthandstories.com/private-equity-pillage.

3 David Robinson, 'Union vote on pension deal clears a big hurdle for Tops Markets', *The Buffalo News*, 10 August 2018, https://buffalonews.com/2018/08/10/union-vote-on-pension-deal-clears-a-big-hurdle-for-tops-markets.

4 Appelbaum and Batt, 'Private'.

5 Appelbaum and Batt, 'Private'.

6 Madison Marquardt, 'Tops union employees approve new contract provisions', *Spectrum Local News*, 9 August 2018, https://spectrumlocalnews.com/nys/rochester/news/2018/08/08/tops-pension-401k-union-vote#.

7 Gerald Epstein, *Financialization and the World Economy* (Cheltenham: Edward Elgar, 2005), 3.

8 Tony Norfield, *The City: London and the Global Power of Finance* (London: Verso, 2016).

9 Apostolos Fasianos, Diego Guevara and Christos Pierros, 'Have we been here before? Phases of financialization within the 20th century in the United States', *Economics Working Paper Archive, Levy Economics Institute*, 2016, https://ideas.repec.org/p/lev/wrkpap/wp_869.html.

10 Victoria Chick, 'The current banking crisis in the UK: an evolutionary view', in *Financial Crises and the Nature of Capitalist Money: Mutual Developments from the Work of Geoffrey Ingham*, ed. Jocelyn Pixley and G. C. Harcourt (London: Palgrave Macmillan, 2013), 148–61.

11 Leo Panitch and Sam Gindin, *The Making of Global Capitalism: The Political Economy of American Empire* (London: Verso, 2012).

12 William Tabb, 'Financialization in the contemporary social structure of accumulation', in *Contemporary Capitalism and Its Crises: Social Structure of Accumulation Theory for the 21st Century*, ed. Terrence McDonough, Michael Reich and David Kotz (Cambridge: Cambridge University Press, 2010), 151.

13 U.S. Bureau of Economic Analysis, 'GDP by industry accounts', last modified 11 December 2019, Table 5a, https://www.bea.gov/data/gdp/gdp-industry; Bureau of Economic Analysis, U.S. Department of Commerce, 'Historical industry accounts data', last modified 31 August 2018, Table 72SIC_VA, GO, II, https://www.bea.gov/industry/io-histannual.

14 Andrew Smith, 'Fast money: the battle against the high frequency traders', *The Guardian*, 7 June 2014, https://www.theguardian.com/business/2014/jun/07/inside-murky-world-high-frequency-trading.
15 Gauti Eggertsson, Jacob Robbins and Ella Getz Wold, 'Kaldor and Piketty's facts: the rise of monopoly power in the United States', NBER Working Papers, 12 February 2018, Table 1. The authors refer to income from rent-seeking as 'pure profits'.
16 Grace Blakeley, 'Introduction', in *Stolen: How to Save the World from Financialization* (London: Repeater Books, 2019).
17 International Labour Organization (ILO) and OECD, 'The labour share in G20 economies', Report prepared for the G20 Employment Working Group, 26–7 February 20156 (Figure 3), https://www.oecd.org/g20/topics/employment-and-social-policy/The-Labour-Share-in-G20-Economies.pdf.
18 International Monetary Fund (IMF), 'World economic outlook, April 2017: gaining momentum?', April 2017, https://www.imf.org/en/Publications/WEO/Issues/2017/04/04/world-economic-outlook-april-2017.
19 Duncan McCann and Christine Berry, 'Shareholder capitalism', *New Economics Foundation*, July 2017, https://neweconomics.org/uploads/files/NEF_SHAREHOLDER-CAPITALISM_E_latest.pdf; Andrew Haldane, 'Who owns a company?', Speech at the University of Edinburgh Corporate Finance Conference, Edinburgh, 22 May 2015, https://www.bis.org/review/r150811a.pdf.
20 William Lazonick, 'Stock buybacks: from retain-and-reinvest to downsize-and-distribute', Report, Centre for Effective Public Management at Brookings, April 2015, 22.
21 Robin Blackburn, 'Finance and the fourth dimension', *New Left Review*, 39 (June 2006), https://newleftreview.

org/issues/II39/articles/robin-blackburn-finance-and-the-fourth-dimension.

22 'Ocado boss Tim Steiner bags £54m bonus', *BBC News*, 11 February 2020, https://www.bbc.co.uk/news/business-51469002.

23 Rana Foroohar, *Makers and Takers: How Wall Street Destroyed Main Street* (New York: Crown, 2016), 124.

24 John Kay, 'The City serves only itself. This is how it could serve us all', *The Telegraph*, 9 September 2015, https://www.telegraph.co.uk/finance/personalfinance/investing/11852003/The-City-serves-only-itself.-This-is-how-it-could-serve-us-all.html.

25 Tim Weber, 'Running a business the Welch way', *BBC News Online*, last modified 26 September 2005, http://news.bbc.co.uk/1/hi/business/4275102.stm.

26 Sarah Anderson, Chuck Collins, Sam Pizzigati, and Kevin Shih, 'CEO pay and the great recession: 17th Annual Executive Compensation Survey', *Institute for Policy Studies*, 1 September 2010, https://ips-dc.org/wp-content/uploads/2010/09/EE-2010-web.pdf.

27 Adam Leaver, 'Out of time: the fragile temporality of Carillion's accumulation model', *SPERI*, 17 January 2018, http://speri.dept.shef.ac.uk/2018/01/17/out-of-time-the-fragile-temporality-of-carillions-accumulation-model.

28 Riccardo Pariboni and Pasquale Tridico, 'Labour share decline, financialization and structural change', *Cambridge Journal of Economics*, 43: 4 (July 2019), https://doi.org/10.1093/cje/bez025.

29 Blackburn, 'Finance'.

30 Greg Ip, 'Credit window: alternative lenders buoy the economy but also pose risk', 11 June 2002, https://gregip.wordpress.com/2002/06/10/credit-window-alternative-lenders-buoy-the-economy-but-also-pose-risk; Ken-Hou

Lin and Donald Tomaskovic-Devey, 'Financialization and U.S. Income Inequality, 1970–2008', *American Journal of Sociology*, 118: 5 (2013), https://doi.org/10.1086/669499.

31 Rana Foroohar, 'Too many businesses want a piece of the financial action', *Financial Times*, 15 May 2016, https://www.ft.com/content/ed421ea4-1925-11e6-b197-a4af20d5575e.

32 Lin and Tomaskovic-Devey, 'Financialization'.

33 Blackburn, 'Finance'.

34 Peter Wells, 'General Electric to freeze pensions for 20,000 employees', *Financial Times*, 7 October 2019, https://www.ft.com/content/349014da-e8ff-11e9-a240-3b065ef5fc55.

35 Jerry Markham, *A Financial History of Modern U.S. Corporate Scandals: From Enron to Reform* (London: Routledge, 2015), 73.

36 Tobias Adrian and Fabio Natalucci, 'Lower for longer: rising vulnerabilities may put growth at risk', *IMF Blog*, 16 October 2019, https://blogs.imf.org/2019/10/16/lower-for-longer-rising-vulnerabilities-may-put-growth-at-risk.

37 James Crotty, 'The neoliberal paradox: the impact of destructive product market competition and impatient finance on nonfinancial corporations in the neoliberal era', *Review of Radical Political Economics*, 35 (1 February 2005), 276, https://doi.org/10.1177/0486613403255533.

38 Bank of England, 'Understanding and measuring finance for productive investment: a discussion paper,' April 2016, 16, chart 8, https://www.bankofengland.co.uk/-/media/boe/files/paper/2016/understanding-and-measuring-finance-for-productive-investment.

39 Eckhard Hein, 'Finance-dominated capitalism and re-distribution of income: a Kaleckian perspective', *Cambridge Journal of Economics*, 39: 3 (May 2015), https://doi.

org/10.1093/cje/bet038; Eckhard Hein and Christian Schoder, 'Interest rates, distribution and capital accumulation: a post-Kaleckian perspective on the US and Germany', *International Review of Applied Economics*, 25: 6 (November 2011), https://doi.org/10.1080/02692171.2011.557054; George Argitis and Christos Pitelis, 'Monetary policy and the distribution of income: evidence for the United States and the United Kingdom', *Journal of Post Keynesian Economics*, 23: 4 (July 2001), https://doi.org/10.1080/01603477.2001.11490302.

40 Karsten Kohler, Alexander Guschanski and Engelbert Stockhammer, 'The impact of financialization on the wage share: a theoretical clarification and empirical test', *Cambridge Journal of Economics*, 43: 4 (July 2019), https://doi.org/10.1093/cje/bez021.

41 Stephen Bronars and Donald Deere, 'The threat of unionization, the use of debt, and the preservation of shareholder wealth', *The Quarterly Journal of Economics*, 106: 1 (1991), https://doi.org/10.2307/2937914.

42 David Dayen, 'Toys "R" Us workers take on private-equity barons: "you ought to be ashamed"', *The Nation*, 5 June 2018, https://www.thenation.com/article/toys-r-us-workers-take-private-equity-barons-ashamed.

43 Private Equity Stakeholder Project and UFCW, 'Report: private equity greed threatens Safeway workers', 19 November 2019, http://www.ufcw400.org/2019/11/06/report-private-equity-greed-threatens-safeway-workers-retirement.

44 Larry Elliott, 'Trade unions attack "corporate greed" of private equity firms', *The Guardian*, 26 January 2007, https://www.theguardian.com/business/2007/jan/26/privateequity.worldeconomicforum.

45 Trades Union Congress (TUC), 'Private equity: a TUC perspective', 23 May 2007, https://www.tuc.org.uk/research-analysis/reports/private-equity-tuc-perspective.

46 Beecher Tuttle, 'Private equity firms dramatically increasing pay as recruiting heats up', *eFinancial Careers*, 14 November 2018, https://news.efinancialcareers.com/us-en/328287/private-equity-firms-dramatically-increasing-pay-recruiting-heats.
47 Research for Action, 'Debt and democracy in Newham: a citizen audit of LOBO debt', 31 October 2018, 44, https://researchforaction.uk/debt-and-democracy-in-newham-a-citizen-audit-of-lobo-debt.
48 Gerald Davis and Suntae Kim, 'Financialization of the economy', *Annual Review of Sociology*, 41 (2015), 16.
49 Stephen Lerner and Jono Shaffer, '25 years later: lessons from the organizers of Justice for Janitors', *The Nation*, 16 June 2015, https://www.thenation.com/article/25-years-later-lessons-from-the-organizers-of-justice-for-janitors.
50 Christina Springer, 'One industry, one union, one contract: how Justice for Janitors organized the invisible', UCLA Department of History, https://www.labor.ucla.edu/wp-content/uploads/2015/03/SPRINGER-160108-Justice-for-Janitors.pdf.
51 Aeron Davis and Catherine Walsh, 'The role of the state in the financialization of the UK economy', *Political Studies*, 63: 3 (2016), 20, http://dx.doi.org/10.1111/1467-9248.12198.
52 The Smith Institute, 'Outsourcing the cuts: pay and employment effects of contracting out', Report, September 2014, 6, https://smithinstitutethinktank.files.wordpress.com/2014/09/outsourcing-the-cuts-pay-and-employment-effects-of-contracting-out.pdf.
53 United Voices of the World, 'St Mary's NHS Hospital staff', accessed 11 March 2020, https://www.uvwunion.org.uk/st-marys-hospital.
54 Jeremy Brecher 'There's still power in a strike', interview with Mark Engler, *Jacobin*, 24 April 2019,

https://jacobinmag.com/2019/04/strike-jeremy-brecher-interview-teachers.

55 John Burant, 'Collective bargaining with the one percent', unpublished working paper, 21, available on request.

56 Howard Reed and Jacob Mohun Himmelweit, 'Where have all the wages gone? Lost pay and profits outside financial services', Touchstone Extras, TUC, 2012, https://www.tuc.org.uk/sites/default/files/tucfiles/where_have_all_the_wages_gone_touchstone_extras_2012.pdf; Matthew Whittaker and Lee Savage, 'Missing out: why ordinary workers are experiencing growth without gain'', *Resolution Foundation*, July 2011, https://www.resolutionfoundation.org/publications/missing.

57 Andrew Haldane, 'The contribution of the financial sector – miracle or mirage', Speech at the Future of Finance conference, 14 July 2010, https://www.bis.org/review/r100716g.pdf, 16.

58 Office for National Statistics (ONS), 'Gross domestic product, preliminary estimate – January to March 2018', 27 April 2018, https://www.ons.gov.uk/economy/grossdomesticproductgdp/bulletins/grossdomesticproductpreliminaryestimate/januarytomarch2018.

59 Alice Martin, Tony Greenham and Helen Kersley. 'Inequality and financialisation: a dangerous mix', Report, New Economics Foundation, 18 December 2014, https://neweconomics.org/2014/12/inequality-and-financialisation.

60 Burant, 'Collective'.

61 Mark DeCambre, 'U.S. consumer debt is now above levels hit during the 2008 financial crisis', *MarketWatch*, 25 June 2019, https://www.marketwatch.com/story/us-consumer-debt-is-now-breaching-levels-last-reached-during-the-2008-financial-crisis-2019-06-19; Maya Goodfellow, 'Britain is crippled by record personal debt while the Tories boast of a boom', *The Guardian*, 7 January 2019,

https://www.theguardian.com/commentisfree/2019/jan/07/britain-personal-debt-tories-uk-households-employment.

62 Graham Hodgson, 'Banking, finance and income inequality', *PositiveMoney*, 2013, http://positivemoney.org/wp-content/uploads/2013/10/Banking-Finance-and-Income-Inequality.pdf.

63 Susanne Soederberg, *Debtfare States and the Poverty Industry: Money, Discipline and the Surplus Population* (Abingdon: Routledge, 2014).

64 Jo Grady and Melanie Simms, 'Trade unions and the challenge of fostering solidarities in an era of financialization', *Economic and Industrial Democracy*, 23 March 2018, 12.

65 David Dayen, 'Payday lenders suffer rare attack of honesty', *The American Prospect*, 11 November 2019, https://prospect.org/api/content/ab83d81e-0237-11ea-b3a3-1244d5f7c7c6.

66 Hari Kishan and Rahul Karunakar, 'U.S. house prices to rise at twice the speed of inflation and pay: Reuters poll', 6 June 2018, https://www.reuters.com/article/us-usa-property-poll/u-s-house-prices-to-rise-at-twice-the-speed-of-inflation-and-pay-reuters-poll-idUSKCN1J20G3; Patrick Collinson, 'UK house prices rising faster than wage increase, Halifax says', *The Guardian*, 7 August 2018, https://www.theguardian.com/money/2018/aug/07/cost-of-buying-a-home-at-record-high-according-to-halifax.

67 Georgetown University, 'The Uber workplace in D.C.', Report, *Georgetown University Kalmanovitz Initiative for Labor and the Working Poor*, 2019, http://lwp.georgetown.edu/wp-content/uploads/Uber-Workplace.pdf.

68 Izabella Kaminska, 'Who really benefits from the growth of self-employment?', *Financial Times*, 28 October 2016,

https://ftalphaville.ft.com/2016/10/28/2178343/who-really-benefits-from-the-growth-of-self-employment.

69 Kaminska, 'Who really benefits'.

70 'Partner Protection insurance with AXA XL in the UK', *Uber.com*, accessed 16 November 2019, https://www.uber.com/gb/en/drive/insurance.

71 'Bank of mum and dad "one of UK's biggest mortgage lenders"', *BBC News*, 27 August 2019, https://www.bbc.com/news/business-49477404.

72 Eggertsson et al., 'Kaldor and Piketty's facts'.

73 Nikou Asgari, 'One in five UK baby boomers are millionaires', *Financial Times*, 9 January 2019, https://www.ft.com/content/c69b49de-1368-11e9-a581-4ff78404524e.

74 Jo Blanden, Paul Gregg and Stephen Machin, 'Intergenerational mobility in Europe and North America: a report supported by the Sutton Trust', Centre for Economic Performance, London School of Economics and Political Science, 1 January 2005.

75 Fabrice Murtin and Mira d'Ercole, 'Household wealth inequality across OECD countries: new OECD evidence', *OECD Statistics Brief*, 21 (2015).

76 Mark Carney, 'A fine balance', Speech given at the Mansion House, London, 20 June 2017, http://www.bankofengland.co.uk/publications/Documents/speeches/2017/speech983.pdf.

77 Christine Berry and Joe Guinan, *People Get Ready! Preparing for a Corbyn Government* (London: OR Books, 2019), 81.

78 Dirk Bezemer, Josh Ryan-Collins, Frank van Lerven and L. Xhang, 'Credit where it's due: a historical, theoretical and empirical review of credit guidance policies in the 20th century', UCL Institute for Innovation and Public Purpose Working Paper 11, 2018.

79 Chris Rhodes, 'Manufacturing: statistics and policy',

House of Commons Library, 10 January 2020, https://commonslibrary.parliament.uk/research-briefings/sn01942.

80 Jane McAlevey, *A Collective Bargain: Unions, Organizing, and the Fight for Democracy* (New York: HarperCollins, 2020).

81 Kim Moody, *Workers in a Lean World: Unions in the International Economy* (London: Verso, 1997), 75.

82 Moody, *Workers*, 10–11.

83 Jason Hickel and Giorgos Kallis, 'Is green growth possible?', *New Political Economy*, 17 April 2019.

84 Beth Stratford, 'The threat of rent extraction in a resource-constrained future', *Ecological Economics*, 169 (2020).

Chapter 2 Understanding and rebuilding union power

1 Bernie Sanders, 'The workplace democracy plan', *Bernie 2020*, accessed 9 March, 2020, https://berniesanders.com/issues/workplace-democracy.

2 UK Labour Party, 'It's time for real change: the Labour Party Manifesto 2019', 59-62, https://labour.org.uk/wp-content/uploads/2019/11/Real-Change-Labour-Manifesto-2019.pdf.

3 Christine Berry and Joe Guinan, *People Get Ready! Preparing for a Corbyn Government* (London: OR Books, 2019).

4 Interview with author, 2019.

5 Jane McAlevey, *No Shortcuts: Organizing for Power in the New Gilded Age* (New York: Oxford University Press, 2016).

6 Donna McGuire, 'Analysing union power, opportunity and strategic capability: global and local union struggles against the General Agreement on Trade in Services (GATS)', *Global Labour Journal*, 5: 1 (2014).

7 Eric Olin Wright, 'Working-class power, capitalist-class

interests and class compromise', *American Journal of Sociology*, 105:4 (2000).

8 Jelle Visser, 'The rise and fall of industrial unionism', *Transfer: European Review of Labour and Research*, 18: 2 (May 2012), 131.

9 Visser, 'Rise', 131.

10 Visser, 'Rise', 131.

11 Visser, 'Rise', 131.

12 Mary Davis, *Comrade or Brother?: A History of the British Labour Movement*, 2nd rev. edn (London: Pluto Press, 2009), 75, 115–16.

13 Ralph Darlington, 'Strike waves, union growth and the rank-and-file/bureaucracy interplay: Britain 1889–1890, 1910–1913 and 1919–1920', *Labor History*, 55: 1 (2014), 3, http://dx.doi.org/10.1080/0023656X.2013.871476.

14 Davis, *Comrade*, 116.

15 John Lovell, '1889: socialism and new unionism', in *British Trade Unions 1875–1933* (London: Macmillan, 1977), 20.

16 William English Walling, 'British and American trade unionism', *The Annals of the American Academy of Political and Social Science*, 26, (November 1905).

17 Marion Dutton Savage, *Industrial Unionism in America* (New York: Ronald Press, 1922), 14–16 and 21–2.

18 Rebecca Gumbrell-McCormick and Richard Hyman, 'Democracy in trade unions, democracy through trade unions?', *Economic and Industrial Democracy*, 24 August 2018, 4; Visser, 'Rise', 133.

19 Jefferson Cowie and Nick Salvatore, 'The long exception: rethinking the place of the New Deal in American history', *Cornell University ILR School Digital Commons* (Fall 2008), 7, https://core.ac.uk/download/pdf/144982701.pdf.

20 Willy Brown, Alex Bryson and John Forth, 'Competition and the retreat from collective bargaining', NIESR Discussion Paper 318 (August 2008), 26.

21 Brown et al., 'Competition'.
22 International Labour Organization (ILO) and OECD, 'The labour share in G20 economies', Report prepared for the G20 Employment Working Group, 26–7 February 2015, 15 (Annex B), https://www.oecd.org/g20/topics/employment-and-social-policy/The-Labour-Share-in-G20-Economies.pdf; Aidan Harper and Alice Martin, 'Working time in UK manufacturing: review of evidence' (New Economics Foundation, forthcoming).
23 Megan Dunn and James Walker, 'Union membership in the United States', *U.S. Bureau Of Labor Statistics*, September 2016, https://www.bls.gov/spotlight/2016/union-membership-in-the-united-states/.
24 Visser, 'Rise', 132.
25 Bernard Ebbinghaus and Jelle Visser, *The Societies of Europe: Trade Unions in Western Europe since 1945* (London: Macmillan, 2000), 62.
26 Cowie and Salvatore 'Long exception', 14.
27 Cowie and Salvatore, 'Long exception', 14.
28 Doug Piper, 'Trade union legislation 1979–2010', House of Commons Briefing Paper 7882, 26 January 2017.
29 Tonia Novitz, 'A revised role for trade unions as designed by New Labour: the representation pyramid and "partnership"', *Journal of Law and Society*, 29: 3 (September 2002), 488–9.
30 Brown et al., 'Competition', 9.
31 Interview with author, 2020
32 T. Raleigh, 'Adapting to a union-free environment', *Wall Street Journal*, 22 October 1984, quoted in John Logan, 'The union avoidance industry in the United States', *British Journal of Industrial Relations*, 44: 4 (December 2006), 654.
33 Logan, 'Union avoidance', 651–2.
34 Robert Smith, 'The business community's mercenaries:

strikebreakers and union busters', in *The Encyclopedia of Strikes in American History*, ed. Aaron Brenner, Benjamin Day and Immanuel Ness (New York: M. E. Sharpe, 2009), 63.

35 Keith Ewing, *Ruined Lives: Blacklisting in the UK Construction Industry* (Liverpool: Institute of Employment Rights, 2009), 1–3.

36 Author's own calculation, based on Office for National Statistics (ONS) figures, https://www.ons.gov.uk/employmentandlabourmarket/peopleinwork/workplacedisputesandworkingconditions/articles/labourdisputes/2018#annual-changes.

37 Özlem Onaran, Alexander Guschanski, James Meadway and Alice Martin, 'Working for the economy: the economic case for trade unions', Policy Brief, New Economics Foundation and University of Greenwich, August 2015, 15–16.

38 Onaran et al., 'Working', 15–16.

39 Brown et al., 'Competition', 18–19.

40 Alan Manning, 'The UK's national minimum wage', *CentrePiece* (Autumn 2009).

41 Stephen Machin and Alan Manning, 'The effects of minimum wages on wage dispersion and employment: evidence from the UK Wage Councils', *Industrial and Labor Relations Review*, 47: 2 (January 1994).

42 Harry Katz, 'The collective bargaining system in the United States: the legacy and the lessons', *Cornell University ILR School Digital Commons* (1998), 20, 150.

43 Brigham Frandsen, 'Why unions still matter: the effects of unionization on the distribution of employee earnings', MIT, 30 January 2012, 29–30, https://economics.mit.edu/files/6950.

44 Frank Manzo and Robert Bruno, 'The impact of "right-to-work" laws on labor market outcomes in three Midwest states: evidence from Indiana, Michigan, and Wisconsin

(2010–2016)', Report for Project for Middle-Class Renewal: Labor Education Program, School of Labor and Employment Relations, 3 April 2017, 3, https://ler.illinois.edu/wp-content/uploads/2017/03/RTW-in-the-Midwest-2010-2016.pdf.

45 Lance Compa, 'An overview of collective bargaining in the United States', *Cornell University ILR School Digital Commons* (2014), 10, 92.

46 Compa, 'Overview'.

47 Gumbrell-McCormick and Hyman, 'Democracy', 2.

48 Dylan Matthews, 'Governors in these states can give workers a raise with the stroke of a pen', *Vox*, 19 July 2019, https://www.vox.com/future-perfect/2019/7/19/20698079/wage-boards-union-labor-movement-california-colorado-new-jersey.

49 Larry Cohen, 'The time has come for sectoral bargaining', *Institute of Employment Rights*, 27 June 2018, https://www.ier.org.uk/blog/time-has-come-sectoral-bargaining.

50 '2019 minimum wage by state', *NCSL*, accessed 18 November 2019, http://www.ncsl.org/research/labor-and-employment/state-minimum-wage-chart.aspx#Table.

51 Interview with author, 2019.

52 Department for Business, Energy & Industrial Strategy, 'Trade union membership statistics 2018', *Trade Union Membership: Statistical Bulletin*, 30 May 2019, https://assets.publishing.service.gov.uk/government/uploads/system/uploads/attachment_data/file/805268/trade-union-membership-2018-statistical-bulletin.pdf; Bureau of Labor Statistics, U.S. Department of Labor, 'News release: union members, 2019', 22 January 2020, https://www.bls.gov/news.release/pdf/union2.pdf.

53 New Economics Foundation, 'Youth membership of unions grows amidst decades of decline', press release, 30 May 2019, https://neweconomics.org/2019/05/

next-generation-of-union-members-drops-by-half-in-10-years.

54 John Schmitt, 'Biggest gains in union membership in 2017 were for younger workers', *Economic Policy Institute*, 25 January 2018, https://www.epi.org/publication/biggest-gains-in-union-membership-in-2017-were-for-younger-workers.

55 Author interview with UK union organizer, 2019.

56 Phoebe Moore, Martin Upchurch and Xanthe Whittaker, *Humans and Machines at Work: Monitoring, Surveillance and Automation in Contemporary Capitalism* (London: Palgrave, 2018), 2–5.

57 Interview with author, 2019.

58 Author interview with UK union organizer, 2019.

59 Stephen Ashe, 'Why I'm talking to white trade unionists about racism', *OpenDemocracy*, 6 September 2019, https://www.opendemocracy.net/en/opendemocracyuk/why-im-talking-white-trade-unionists-about-racism.

60 Melanie Simms, 'Trade union responses to precarious work: UK report', BARSORI Research Report, 2011, 24, http://eprints.gla.ac.uk/190821.

61 Interview with author, 2019.

62 United Voices of the World (UVW), 'St Mary's Workers', accessed 9 March 2020, https://www.uvwunion.org.uk/stmarysworkers.

63 European Trade Union Institute (ETUI), 'France', *worker-participation.eu*, accessed 18 November 2019, https://www.worker-participation.eu/National-Industrial-Relations/Countries/France.

64 Martin Vranken, 'Labour law reform in France: the Macron effect', Victoria University of Wellington, 24, https://www.wgtn.ac.nz/__data/assets/pdf_file/0016/1700251/Vranken.pdf.

65 Heather Connolly, *Renewal in the French Trade Union*

Movement: A Grassroots Perspective (New York: Peter Lang, 2010), 39–42.

66 Magdalena Bernaciak, Rebecca Gumbrell-Mccormick and Richard Hyman, 'Trade unions in Europe: innovative responses to hard times', *Friedrich Ebert Stiftung*, April 2014, 1–2, https://library.fes.de/pdf-files/id-moe/10688.pdf, 1–2.

67 ETUI, 'The European Participation Index (EPI): a tool for cross-national quantitative comparison', *worker-participation.eu*, 2010, accessed 9 April 2020, https://www.worker-participation.eu/About-WP/European-Participation-Index-EPI/The-European-Participation-Index-measuring-worker-participation-and-Europe-2020-targets.

68 Jens Kristiansen, 'European challenges of the Nordic collective-agreement model', in *Europe and the Nordic Collective-Bargaining Model*, ed. Jens Kristiansen (Copenhagen: Nordic Council of Ministers, 2015), 16–17.

69 Søren Kaj Andersen, Jon Erik Dølvik and Christian Lyhne Ibsen, 'Nordic labour market models in open markets', *Report 132*, (Brussels: ETUI, 2014), 17, https://www.etui.org/Publications2/Reports/Nordic-labour-market-models-in-open-markets.

70 Andersen et al., 'Nordic', 16.

71 Kristiansen, 'European', 16–17; Andersen et al., 'Nordic'.

72 Gumbrell-McCormick and Hyman, 'Democracy', 2.

73 Sabina Avdagic and Lucio Baccaro, 'The future of employment relations in advanced capitalism', in *The Oxford Handbook of Employment Relations*, ed. Adrian Wilkinson, Geoffrey Wood and Richard Deeg, 1 March 2014, https://doi.org/10.1093/oxfordhb/9780199695096.013.031.

74 Andy Storey, 'The European project: dismantling the social model, globalizing neoliberalism', *The Irish Review*, 34 (Spring 2006).

75 Özlem Onaran and Engelbert Stockhammer, 'Policies for wage-led growth in Europe', FEPS Policy Report, February 2016, https://www.feps-europe.eu/Assets/Publications/PostFiles/364_1.pdf.
76 European Commission, 'The Broad Economic Policy Guidelines (for the 2005–08 Period)', *European Economy*, 5 (2004), 15, https://ec.europa.eu/economy_finance/publications/pages/publication6432_en.pdf.
77 Jelle Visser, 'What happened to collective bargaining during the great recession?', *IZA Journal of Labor Policy*, 5: 9 (2016).
78 Andersen et al., 'Nordic'.
79 Tony Norfield, *The City: London and the Global Power of Finance* (London: Verso, 2016).
80 Rory Tingle, 'Mind the pay gap! London Tube drivers on £100,000-a-year salaries are earning more than airline pilots despite their jobs getting easier as staff who open and close automatic doors earn a 4% hike', 16 December 2018, *Dailymail.com*, https://www.dailymail.co.uk/news/article-6500923/Mind-pay-gap-London-Tube-drivers-100-000-year-salaries-pilots.html.
81 Interview with author, 2020.
82 OECD, 'Inequalities in household wealth across OECD countries: evidence from the OECD Wealth Distribution Database', 20 June 2018, https://www.oecd.org/officialdocuments/publicdisplaydocumentpdf/?cote=SDD/DOC(2018)1&docLanguage=En.
83 Geoffrey Hodgson, 'What the world can learn about equality from the Nordic model', *The Conversation*, 30 July 2018, http://theconversation.com/what-the-world-can-learn-about-equality-from-the-nordic-model-99797.
84 Rolf Aaberge, Christophe André, Anne Boschini et al., *Increasing Income Inequality in the Nordics: Nordic Economic Policy Review 2018*, TemaNord 2018:519

(Copenhagen: Nordic Council of Ministers, 2018), 13, https://doi.org/10.6027/TN2018-519.

85 Thomas Blanchet, Lucas Chancel and Amory Gethin, 'Has the European social model withstood the rise in inequalities?', *World Inequality Lab*, April 2019, https://wid.world/document/european-inequality-wil-summary-2019-en-pdf.

86 Rudolf Meidner, 'Why did the Swedish model fail?', *Socialist Register*, 29 (18 March 1993), 222, https://socialistregister.com/index.php/srv/article/view/5630; Per-Anders Edin and Bertl Holmlund, 'The Swedish wage structure: the rise and fall of solidarity wage policy?', NBER Working Papers, January 1993, https://doi.org/10.3386/w4257.

87 Meidner, 'Why'.

88 Meidner, 'Why', 219.

89 Interview with author, 2019.

90 Alice Martin, Rebecca Winson and Lukazs Krebal, 'Time for democracy', New Economics Foundation (forthcoming).

Chapter 3 Bargaining with finance

1 'Reality check to teachers union: affordable housing has no place at the bargaining table', *Chicago Sun-Times*, 9 October 2019, https://chicago.suntimes.com/2019/10/9/20906492/chicago-teachers-union-contract-talks-affordable-housing-suntimes-editorial.

2 Mike Elk, 'Why does the Chicago teachers union care about interest rate swaps?', *In These Times*, 31 May 2011, http://inthesetimes.com/working/entry/7371/why_does_the_chicago_teachers_union_care_about_interest_rate_swaps.

3 Amisha Patel, 'Op ed: mayor chooses banks over students', *Chicago Teachers Union*, 4 April 2013, https://

www.ctulocal1.org/posts/op-ed-mayor-chooses-banks-over-students.

4 'Chicago teachers union protest of TIFs leads to arrest', *Daily Kos*, 20 March 2011, https://www.dailykos.com/stories/2011/3/20/958230/-.

5 Cassie Walker Burke, 'The fight at the heart of the Chicago teachers strike: how much the city can spend', *Chalkbeat*, 23 October 2019, https://chalkbeat.org/posts/chicago/2019/10/23/at-issue-in-chicago-teachers-strike-how-much-the-city-can-spend.

6 Marnie Brady, 'Workers and renters of the world, unite!', *Jacobin*, September 2019, https://jacobinmag.com/2019/09/rent-control-affordable-housing-teacher-pension-funds-evictions.

7 'The fight for housing stability', *Chicago Teachers Union*, 12 June 2019, https://www.ctulocal1.org/chicago-union-teacher/2019/06/the-fight-for-housing-stability.

8 Mary Davis, *Comrade or Brother? – A History of the British Labour Movement*, 2nd rev. edn (London: Pluto Press, 2009), 61.

9 Malcolm Chase, *Chartism: A New History* (Manchester: Manchester University Press, 2013),305.

10 Judith Stepan-Norris and Maurice Zeitlin, *Left Out: Reds and America's Industrial Unions* (Cambridge: Cambridge University Press, 2003).

11 Jane McAlevey, *No Shortcuts: Organizing for Power in the New Gilded Age* (New York: Oxford University Press, 2016).

12 Brady, 'Workers'.

13 'About us', *Bargaining for the Common Good*, accessed 12 March 2020, http://www.bargainingforthecommongood.org/about.

14 'Unite Community membership', *Unite the Union*, accessed 15 November 2019, https://unitetheunion.org/community.

15 'UCL cleaners and academics to picket together in first ever joint strike', *IWGB*, 3 December 2019, https://iwgb.org.uk/en/post/5de62e27a52e3/ucl-cleaners-and-academi cs-to.
16 Michael Fichter, 'Organising in and along value chains : what does it mean for trade unions?', *Friedrich Ebert Stiftung*, 2015, 14.
17 'Auto unions develop value chain organizing strategies', *IndustriALL*, 9 November 2018, http://www.industriall-union.org/auto-unions-develop-value-chain-organizing-strategies.
18 James Gordon, 'Cobalt mining in the DRC: the dark side of a clean future', *Raconteur*, 3 June 2019, https://www.raconteur.net/business-innovation/cobalt-mining-human-rights.
19 Interview with author, 2019.
20 Interview with author, 2020.
21 Interview with author, 2020.
22 Kim Moody, *On New Terrain: How Capital is Reshaping the Battleground of Class War* (Chicago: Haymarket Books, 2017), 59–65.
23 Moody, *On New Terrain.*
24 McAlevey, *No Shortcuts*, 28.
25 'About us', *Bargaining for the Common Good.*
26 'Saint Paul Public Schools Regular Meeting', 21 June 2016, 114, accessed 12 March 2020, https://www.spps.org/site/handlers/filedownload.ashx?moduleinstanceid=91622&dataid=72550&FileName=062116.pdf.
27 'Committee for Better Banks', *Committee for Better Banks* (blog), accessed 14 October 2019, https://better-banks.org.
28 'Academics, organizers, and activists gather to address bank worker organizing', *Georgetown University Kalmanovitz Initiative for Labor and the Working Poor*, 21 August 2018, http://lwp.georgetown.edu/2018/08/

21/academics-organizers-and-activists-gather-to-address-bank-worker-organizing; Josh Bivens, Lora Engdahl, Elise Gould et al., 'How today's unions help working people: giving workers the power to improve their jobs and unrig the economy', *Economic Policy Institute*, 24 August 2017, https://www.epi.org/publication/how-todays-unions-help-working-people-giving-workers-the-power-to-improve-their-jobs-and-unrig-the-economy.

29 'L.A. bank workers, residents, consumer advocates join city council members in rally to celebrate first-in-the-nation responsibility requirement for banks', *Committee for Better Banks Los Angeles*, 3 July 2018, https://www.betterbanksla.org/news/l-a-bank-workers-residents-consumer-advocates-join-city-council-members-in-rally-to-celebrate-first-in-the-nation-responsibility-requirements-for-banks.

30 Interview in New Economics Foundation workshop with community and union organizers, 2019.

31 Stephen Lerner and Jono Shaffer, '25 years later: lessons from the organizers of Justice for Janitors', *The Nation*, 16 June 2015, https://www.thenation.com/article/25-years-later-lessons-from-the-organizers-of-justice-for-janitors; John B. Howley, 'Justice for Janitors: the challenge of organizing in contract services', 1990, *Cornell University ILR School Digital Commons*, 1: 15 (1990), https://digitalcommons.ilr.cornell.edu/lrr/vol1/iss15/4.

32 Emiliano Mellino, 'IWGB to face government in landmark case to extend rights of outsourced workers', *IWGB*, 12 August 2018, https://iwgb.org.uk/post/5b6f8c7ebb3d8/iwgb-to-face-government-in.

33 International Transport Workers' Federation (ITF), 'Quarter of National Express shareholders defy board over US labour rights', *ITF Global*, 8 May 2015, https://www.itfglobal.org/en/news/quarter-national-express-shareholders-defy-board-over-us-labour-rights.

34 International Brotherhood of Teamsters, 'Teamsters: National Express shareholders call for review of workplace rights', *Teamster*, 9 March 2016.

35 Stewart Schwab and Randall Thomas, 'Realigning corporate governance: shareholder activism by labour unions', *Michigan Law Review* 96 (1998), 1025–7.

36 Tom Powdrill, 'Who's responsible? Pension funds and respect for workers' rights', Report, *International Transport Workers' Federation*, 2017, 6, https://www.itfglobal.org/sites/default/files/resources-files/pension-funds-and-respect-for-workers-rights.pdf.

37 Powdrill, 'Who's responsible?'.

38 David Webber, *The Rise of the Working-Class Shareholder: Labor's Last Best Weapon* (Cambridge MA: Harvard University Press, 2018).

39 Wes Venteicher, 'CalPERS pulls millions of dollars out of immigrant detention companies', *The State Worker*, 21 October 2019, https://www.sacbee.com/news/politics-government/the-state-worker/article236485828.html.

40 Jo Grady, 'Manifesto: 8. Pensions', *Jo Grady for UCU General Secretary*, accessed 12 March 2020, https://grady4gs.com/manifesto/8-pensions.

41 Bob Farkas, 'The mirage of pension-fund activism', *Jacobin*, 16 April 2018, https://www.jacobinmag.com/2018/04/pension-fund-activism-working-class-shareholder-review.

42 'Rolling Jubilee', accessed 15 October 2019, http://rollingjubilee.org.

43 Hannah Appel, 'There is power in a debtor's union', *Dissent*, 12 July 2019, https://www.dissentmagazine.org/online_articles/there-is-power-in-a-debtors-union; Hannah Appel, 'Debtors of the world, unite!', *Boston Review*, 27 February 2020, http://bostonreview.net/class-inequality/hannah-appel-debtors-world-unite.

44 Appel, 'There is power'.

45 Tom Perkins, 'GM strike ends after 40 days with 48,000 staff return to work', *The Guardian*, 25 October 2019, https://www.theguardian.com/business/2019/oct/25/uaw-united-auto-workers-general-motors-strike-deal.
46 Interview with author, 2020.
47 Strike Debt/Occupy Wall Street, *The Debt Resistors' Operations Manual*, September 2012, https://strikedebt.org/The-Debt-Resistors-Operations-Manual.pdf.
48 Stephen Lerner and Saqib Bhatti, 'US: fighting foreclosures, making the banks pay', *Red Pepper*, 23 April 2013, https://www.redpepper.org.uk/us-movement-battles-foreclosures-and-evictions.
49 Mellissa Lamarca, 'Resisting evictions Spanish style', *New Internationalist*, 1 April 2013, https://newint.org/features/2013/04/01/sparks-from-the-spanish-crucible.
50 Sewin Chan, Andrew Haughwout, Andrew Hayashi and Wilbert van der Klaauw, 'Determinants of mortgage default and consumer credit use: the effects of foreclosure laws and foreclosure delays', Federal Reserve Bank of New York Staff Reports 732, June 2015, https://www.newyorkfed.org/medialibrary/media/research/staff_reports/sr732.pdf.
51 Gillian White, 'Sometimes, defaulting on a mortgage is a smart decision', *The Atlantic*, 9 July 2015, https://www.theatlantic.com/business/archive/2015/07/mortgage-default-finances/398051.
52 'Rent strikes: a brief history', *Rent Strike*, accessed 12 March 2020, https://www.rent-strike.org/history.
53 Michael Karp, 'The St. Louis rent strike of 1969: transforming black activism and American low-income housing', *Journal of Urban History*, 40: 4 (2014).
54 Elijah Chiland, 'More than 80 tenants launch multi-building rent strike in Westlake', *Curbed, Los Angeles*, 10 April 2018, https://la.curbed.com/2018/4/10/17216952/westlake-rent-strike-tenants-union-eviction-defense.

55 Rob Kuznia, 'Los Angeles tenants increasingly engaging in rent strikes amid housing crisis', *The Washington Post*, 6 February 2018, https://www.washingtonpost.com/national/los-angeles-tenants-increasingly-engaging-in-rent-strikes-amid-housing-crisis/2018/06/02/6b91c340-65af-11e8-a768-ed043e33f1dc_story.html; Kevin Barry, 'Legal battle between owners and residents of The Vue after Jan. flooding could spill into the summer', *News5Cleveland*, 9 April 2014, https://www.news5cleveland.com/news/e-team/legal-battle-between-owners-and-residents-after-january-flooding-could-spill-into-the-summer.

56 Lillian M. Ortiz, 'Tenant power: organizing for rent strikes and landlord negotiations', *Shelterforce*, 30 July 2018, https://shelterforce.org/2018/07/30/tenant-power-organizing-for-rent-strikes-and-landlord-negotiations.

57 'Parkdale tenants declare victory, end strike saying they've "won" deal with landlord', *CBC News*, 12 August 2017, https://www.cbc.ca/news/canada/toronto/parkdale-rent-strike-ends-1.4245237.

58 Diane Taylor, 'University students across London take part in rent strike', *The Guardian*, 6 May 2016, https://www.theguardian.com/education/2016/may/06/university-students-across-london-take-part-in-rent-strike.

59 Peter Bill, Paul Hackett and Catherine Glossop, 'The future of the private rented sector', (London: Smith Institute, 2008), https://www.bl.uk/britishlibrary/~/media/bl/global/social-welfare/pdfs/non-secure/f/u/t/future-of-the-private-rented-sector.pdf.

60 Interview with housing expert Joe Beswick, 2019.

61 'Sustained collective action pays off big time for Mary!', *London Renters Union*, 24 April 2019, https://londonrentersunion.org/2019/mary-win.

62 'Trades councils: who we are and what we do', *TUC*, accessed 12 March 2020, https://www.tuc.org.uk/trades-councils-who-we-are-and-what-we-do.

63 McAlevey, *No Shortcuts*, 114–19.
64 Interview with author, 2020.
65 Simon Childs, 'How Britain's biggest union undermined the struggles of migrant workers', *Vice*, 13 June 2019, https://www.vice.com/en_uk/article/nea4v8/union-strike-migrant-workers-london-university.
66 Department for Business, Energy and Industrial Strategy (BEIS), 'Trade union membership statistics 2018', *Trade Union Membership: Statistical Bulletin*', 30 May 2018, https://assets.publishing.service.gov.uk/government/uploads/system/uploads/attachment_data/file/805268/trade-union-membership-2018-statistical-bulletin.pdf.
67 Clare Mullaly, 'A woman's place is in her trade union', *TUC*, 8 June 2018, https://www.tuc.org.uk/blogs/womans-place-her-trade-union.
68 Interview with author, 2020.
69 Interview with UK union organizer, 2019.
70 Stephen Ashe, 'Why I'm talking to white trade unionists about racism', *OpenDemocracy*, 6 September 2019, https://www.opendemocracy.net/en/opendemocracyuk/why-im-talking-white-trade-unionists-about-racism.
71 Ashe, 'Why I'm talking'.
72 Jesse Hagopian, 'A people's history of the Chicago Teachers Union', *International Socialist Review*, 86 (May 2009), https://isreview.org/issue/86/peoples-history-chicago-teachers-union.
73 Becki Winson, 'Workers and the world', *Tribune*, 1 May 2019, https://tribunemag.co.uk/2019/05/workers-and-the-world.
74 Damian Carrington, 'School climate strikes: 1.4 million people took part, say campaigners', *The Guardian*, 19 March 2019, https://www.theguardian.com/environment/2019/mar/19/school-climate-strikes-more-than-1-million-took-part-say-campaigners-greta-thunberg.
75 Winson, 'Workers and the world'.

76 Miranda Hall, 'Will apps help carers find decent work?', *New Economics Foundation*, 18 June 2018, https://neweconomics.org/2018/06/will-apps-help-carers-find-decent-work.
77 Unison Scotland, 'Glasgow women's strike: when women come together and take action, we win', 16 April 2019, https://unison-scotland.org/glasgow-womens-strike-when-women-come-together-and-take-action-we-win.
78 Nadine Houghton, 'Working class women in the UK were the unsung heroes of 2016: here are four of their major victories', *The Independent*, 18 December 2016, https://www.independent.co.uk/voices/working-class-women-strikes-victories-in-2016-a7479586.html.

Chapter 4 Owning the future

1 Eva Lloyd and Helen Penn, *Childcare Markets* (Bristol: Policy Press, 2013), 211.
2 Lloyd and Penn, *Childcare Markets*, 210.
3 Lloyd and Penn, *Childcare Markets*.
4 Commonwealth of Australia, 'Provision of childcare', 23 November 2009, ch. 2, https://www.aph.gov.au/Parliamentary_Business/Committees/Senate/Education_Employment_and_Workplace_Relations/Completed_inquiries/2008-10/child_care/report/index.
5 Commonwealth of Australia, 'Provision', ch. 2.
6 Emma Rush and Christian Downie, 'ABC Learning Centres: a case study of Australia's largest child care corporation', Australia Institute Discussion Paper 87, June 2006, https://www.tai.org.au/sites/default/files/DP87_8.pdf.
7 Commonwealth of Australia, 'Provision', ch. 2.
8 Lloyd and Penn, *Childcare Markets*.
9 Commonwealth of Australia, 'Provision', ch. 2.
10 Rush and Downie, 'ABC', 32–5.

11 BusinessSpectator, 'Eddy Groves back in business', *Gold Coast Bulletin*, 23 February 2016, https://www.goldcoastbulletin.com.au/news/eddy-groves-back-in-business/news-story/4eeaa4003db2bf5ad802d0e686fe174f.

12 Helen Penn, 'Why parents should fear childcare going the way of Carillion', *The Guardian*, 4 May 2018, https://www.theguardian.com/commentisfree/2018/may/14/parents-carillion-childcare-collapse-nursery-provider.

13 These ideas are being developed by Lucie Stephens and Miranda Hall at the New Economics Foundation.

14 Mathew Lawrence, Andrew Pendleton and Sara Mahmoud, 'Co-operatives unleashed: doubling the size of the UK's co-operative sector', *New Economics Foundation*, 2018, 2, https://neweconomics.org/uploads/files/co-ops-unleashed.pdf; Edward Wolff, 'Household wealth trends in the United States, 1962 to 2016: has middle class wealth recovered?', NBER Working Papers, November 2017, https://www.nber.org/papers/w24085?utm_campaign=ntw&utm_medium=email&utm_source=ntw.

15 Marjorie Kelly, *Owning Our Future: The Emerging Ownership Revolution* (San Francisco: Berrett–Koehler, 2012).

16 Daron Acemoglu, 'Labor- and capital-augmenting technical change', *Journal of the European Economic Association*, 1:1 (2003); PWC, 'Will robots really steal our jobs? An international analysis of the potential long term impact of automation', 2018, https://www.pwc.co.uk/economic-services/assets/international-impact-of-automation-feb-2018.pdf.

17 Rebecca Gumbrell-McCormick and Richard Hyman, 'Democracy in trade unions, democracy through trade unions?', *Economic and Industrial Democracy*, 24 August 2018, 3.

18 'When we own it: a model for public ownership in the

21st century', *We Own It*, May 2019, https://weownit.org.uk/when-we-own-it.

19 Christine Berry and Joe Guinan, *People Get Ready! Preparing for a Corbyn Government* (London: OR Books, 2019), 48–51, 36.

20 John Medhurst, *That Option No Longer Exists: Britain 1974–76* (Alresford: John Hunt, 2014), 56.

21 Medhurst, *That Option*, 76.

22 UK Labour Party, 'Alternative models of ownership', Report to the Shadow Chancellor of the Exchequer and Shadow Secretary of State for Business, Energy and Industrial Strategy, 2017, https://labour.org.uk/wp-content/uploads/2017/10/Alternative-Models-of-Ownership.pdf .

23 Lawrence et al., 'Co-operatives unleashed'.

24 Rudolf Meidner, 'Why did the Swedish model fail?', *Socialist Register*, 29 (18 March 1993), 224, https://socialistregister.com/index.php/srv/article/view/5630.

25 Meidner, 'Why', 224.

26 Jonas Pontusson and Sarosh Kuruvilla, 'Swedish wage-earner funds: an experiment in economic democracy', *Industrial and Labor Relations Review*, 45: 4 (1992), 785.

27 Jens Lowitzsch, *Financial Participation of Employees in the EU-27* (New York: Palgrave Macmillan, 2009), 306.

28 Nikola Balnave and Greg Patmore, 'The Labour Movement and co-operatives', *Labour History*, 112 (May 2017), 8.

29 Angela Frances Whitecross, 'Co-operative commonwealth or New Jerusalem? The Co-operative Party and the Labour Party,1931–1951', PhD thesis, January 2015, http://clok.uclan.ac.uk/11485/3/Whitecross%20Angela%20Final%20e-Thesis%20%28Master%20Copy%29.pdf.

30 'Sustainable jobs, sustainable communities: the union

co-op model', *Community-Wealth.org*, 21 February 2014, https://community-wealth.org/content/sustainable-jobs-sustainable-communities-union-co-op-model.

31 Gumbrell-McCormick and Hyman, 'Democracy'.

32 Marina Monaco and Luca Pastorelli, 'Trade unions and worker cooperatives in Europe: a win–win relationship', International Labor Movement Meeting Document 3, accessed 12 March 2020, 3, http://www.ilo.org/wcmsp5/groups/public/---ed_dialogue/---actrav/documents/meetingdocument/wcms_234169.pdf.

33 Rob Witherell, Chris Cooper and Michael Peck, 'Sustainable jobs, sustainable communities: the union co-op model', *Community-Wealth.org*, March 2012, https://community-wealth.org/content/sustainable-jobs-sustainable-communities-union-co-op-model; Laura Hanson Schlachter, 'Stronger together? The USW-Mondragon Union co-op model', University of Wisconsin-Madison, September 2016, 9.

34 Amy Dean, 'Why unions are going into the co-op business', *Yes!*, 6 March 2013, https://www.yesmagazine.org/issues/how-co-operatives-are-driving-the-new-economy/union-co-ops.

35 Stu Schneider, 'Cooperative Home Care Associates: participation with 1600 employees', 20 April 2010, http://www.geo.co-op/node/433.

36 Jay Cassano, 'Inside America's largest worker-run business', *Fast Company*, 8 September 2015, https://www.fastcompany.com/3049930/inside-americas-largest-worker-run-business.

37 Cassano, 'Inside'.

38 Lawrence et al., 'Co-operatives unleashed', 4.

39 Tim Palmer, '2017 worker cooperative state of the sector report', *Democracy at Work Institute*, 18 December 2019, https://institute.coop/resources/2017-worker-cooperative-state-sector-report.

40 Palmer, '2017 worker cooperative'.
41 Lawrence et al., 'Co-operatives unleashed'.
42 Elli Anzilotti, 'More US businesses are becoming worker co-ops. Here's why', *Fast Company*, 21 May 2018, https://www.fastcompany.com/40572926/more-u-s-businesses-are-becoming-worker-co-ops-heres-why
43 Jane Slaughter, 'Republic Windows sit-downers become worker owners', *Labor Notes*, 9 May 2013 https://www.labornotes.org/2013/05/republic-windows-sit-downers-become-worker-owners.
44 Unite the Union, 'Defence diversification revisited', May 2016, 13, https://unitetheunion.org/media/1108/unite-diversification-revisited.pdf.
45 Unite the Union, 'Defence'.
46 Unite the Union, 'Defence'.
47 Pritti Mistry, 'End of an era for BAE aircraft manufacturing in Brough', *BBC News*, 1 March 2012, https://www.bbc.com/news/uk-england-humber-17217413.
48 Marcelo Vieta, 'Saving jobs and businesses in times of crisis: the Italian road to creating more worker buy-outs', in *Cooperatives and the World of Work*, ed. Bruno Roelants, Hyungsik Eum, Simel Eşim et al. (New York: Routledge, 2020).
49 Vieta, 'Saving jobs'.
50 Roberto Cardinale, Chiara Migliorini and Francesca Zarri, 'Italian social cooperatives and trade unions in the crisis era', ILO and Generazioni Legacoop Emilia Romagna, January 2014, 6, https://www.ilo.org/wcmsp5/groups/public/---ed_dialogue/---actrav/documents/meetingdocument/wcms_234159.pdf.
51 Cardinale et al., 'Italian social cooperatives'.
52 Author interview with Emily Scurrah, New Economics Foundation, 2019.
53 International Domestic Workers Federation (IDWFED), 'India: Self Employed Women's Association (SEWA)', 17

September 2014, https://idwfed.org/en/affiliates/asia-pacific/sewa.

54 Jaya Arunachalam, *Women's Equality: A Struggle for Survival* (New Delhi: Gyan, 2005), 72.

55 Justin Bentham, Andrew Bowman, Marta de la Cuesta et al., 'Manifesto for the foundational economy', CRESC Working Paper 131, November 2013, https://hummedia.manchester.ac.uk/institutes/cresc/workingpapers/wp131.pdf.

56 Andrew Bowman, Ismail Ertürk, Julie Froud, Sukhdev Johal and John Law, *The End of the Experiment? From Competition to the Foundational Economy* (Manchester: Manchester University Press: 2014).

57 Office of Science and Technology Policy, The White House, 'America will dominate the industries of the future', 7 February 2019, https://www.whitehouse.gov/briefings-statements/america-will-dominate-industries-future; Department for Business, Energy and Industrial Strategy (BEIS), 'Industrial strategy: building a Britain fit for the future', Policy Paper, *GOV.UK*, last updated 28 June 2018, https://www.gov.uk/government/publications/industrial-strategy-building-a-britain-fit-for-the-future.

58 Stephen Devlin, '(In)equality in the digital society: – Workshop summary', New Economics Foundation and Friedrich-Ebert-Stiftung London, 2017, https://www.fes-london.org/fileadmin/user_upload/publications/files/Inequality-in-the-Digital-Society-Workshop-Summary.pdf.

59 Theresa May, 'PM speech on science and modern industrial strategy: 21 May 2018', *GOV.UK*, 21 May 2018, https://www.gov.uk/government/speeches/pm-speech-on-science-and-modern-industrial-strategy-21-may-2018.

60 Devlin, '(In)equality'.

61 David Powell, Fernanda Balata, Frank Van Lerven and Margaret Welsh, 'Trust in transition, climate breakdown

and high carbon workers', Report, *New Economics Foundation*, https://neweconomics.org/2019/11/trust-in-transition.

62 National Audit Office, 'The privatisation of Royal Mail: – press release', 31 March 2014, https://www.nao.org.uk/press-release/privatisation-royal-mail.

63 Author interview with Andrew Towers, head of political strategy, CWU, 2019.

64 Erik Forman, 'How unions can solve the housing crisis', *In These Times*, 23 September–October 2018, http://inthesetimes.com/features/unions-housing-crisis-labor-co-op-apartments-new-york-homeless-rent-control.html.

65 Forman, 'How unions'.

66 Amalgamated Bank, 'America's socially responsible bank', accessed 10 March 2020, https://www.amalgamatedbank.com/who-we-are.

67 Forman, 'How unions'.

68 Cincinnati Union Co-op, 'Renting partnerships', accessed 22 November 2019, https:// coopcincy.org/renting-partnerships.

69 Lucas Aerospace Combine Shop Steward Committee, 'Corporate plan: a contingency strategy as a positive alternative to recession and redundancies', 1976, 6, https://www.dropbox.com/s/o2sqxvhams2ywup/Lucas-Plan-53pp-alternative%20corporate%20plan.pdf?dl=0.

70 Hilary Wainwright and Dave Elliott, *The Lucas Plan: A New Trade Unionism in the Making?* (Nottingham: Spokesman Books, 2018), 1–3.

71 Lucas Aerospace Combine Shop Steward Committee, 'Corporate plan', 5.

72 *Financial Times*, 23 January 1976, cited in Hilary Wainwright and Dave Elliott, *The Lucas Plan: A New Trade Unionism in the Making?* (London: Allison and Busby, 1982), 140.

73 Adrian Smith, 'Socially useful production', STEPS Working Paper 58, *STEPS Centre*, 2014, 15.

74 Phil Asquith, 'Bang on target: a brief union history of arms conversion', *Red Pepper*, 11 September 2015, https://www.redpepper.org.uk/bang-on-target-a-brief-union-history-of-arms-conversion.

75 Asquith, 'Bang on target'.

76 Edward Ongweso Jr 'General Electric workers expand protests, now demand to make ventilators nationwide', *Vice*, 8 April, 2020, https://www.vice.com/en_us/article/7kzy8z/general-electric-workers-expand-protests-now-demand-to-make-ventilators-nationwide.

77 CWA News, 'IEU-CWA members increase pressure on GE to boost ventilator production and enhance safety', 9 April 2020, https://cwa-union.org/news/iue-cwa-members-increase-pressure-on-ge-boost-ventilator-production-and-enhance-safety.

78 GMB Scotland, 'Overview: battle for BiFab', accessed 10 March 2020, https://www.gmbscotland.org.uk/campaigns/battle-for-bifab/overview.

79 Douglas Fraser, 'BiFab "loses out" on "vital" wind farm contract', *BBC News*, 7 March 2019. https://www.bbc.co.uk/news/uk-scotland-scotland-business-47478083; David McPhee, 'BiFab yard to be mothballed despite firm cutting losses by £42m', *Energy Voice*, 20 December 20.

80 Rob Davies, 'Harland and Wolff saved from closure in £6m rescue deal', *The Guardian*, 1 October 2019, https://www.theguardian.com/business/2019/oct/01/harland-and-wolff-saved-from-closure-in-6m-rescue-deal.

81 David H. Autor and David Dorn, 'The growth of low-skill service jobs and the polarization of the US labor market', *American Economic Review*, 103: 5 (2013); PWC, 'Will robots'.

82 Carys Roberts, Henry Parkes, Rachel Statham and Lesley

Rankin, 'The future is ours: women, automation and equality', *IPPR*, 16 July 2019, 56, https://www.ippr.org/research/publications/women-automation-and-equality; ONS, 'The probability of automation in England: 2011 and 2017', https://www.ons.gov.uk/employmentandlabourmarket/peopleinwork/employmentandemployeetypes/articles/theprobabilityofautomationinengland/2011and2017.

83 Author interview with Fórsa union official, 2019.

84 Aidan Harper, 'Achieving a shorter working week across Europe', *European Network for the Fair Sharing of Working Time Newsletter*, 1–4, March–December 2019, https://neweconomics.org/campaigns/euro-working-time; Aidan Harper and Alice Martin, 'Shorter working hours in manufacturing: a review of evidence', New Economics Foundation and Confederation of Engineering and Shipbuilding Unions, forthcoming.

85 Author interview with UK union officials from the Confederation of Shipbuilding and Engineering Unions (CSEU) and Unite the Union, 2019.

86 Helen Hester and Nick Srnicek, *After Work: The Fight for Free Time* (London, Verso, 2020).

87 Interview with author, 2019.

88 Anton Jager, 'Why "post-work" doesn't work', *Jacobin*, November 2018, https://www.jacobinmag.com/2018/11/post-work-ubi-nick-srnicek-alex-williams.

89 David Graeber, *Bullshit Jobs: A Theory* (New York: Simon and Schuster, 2018).

Conclusion: a way forward

1 ICNARC, 'ICNARC report on COVID-19 in critical care', 10 April 2020, https://www.icnarc.org/About/Latest-News/2020/04/04/Report-On-2249-Patients-Critically-Ill-With-Covid-19/; Fabiola Cineas, 'Covid-19 is

disproportionately taking black lives,' *Vox*, 8 April 2020, https://www.vox.com/identities/2020/4/7/21211849/coronavirus-black-americans.